Text written
in association with
Michèle Aué

Translated by Juliette Freyche

CATHAR COUNTRY

LE PAYS CATHARE

MSM

≈

SUMMARY

Map 4-5

History 7

The country and its destiny 9
The Cathar Religion, a dualist Christianity 11
The Cathar Tragedy 15

Itineraries 47

The Albigeois, Toulousain and Lauragais Areas 49
The Ariege Area 65
Quercorb, Corbières and Razès 79
Carcassès, Cabardès, Minervois, Béziers and Narbonne 107

Index 128

Itineraries

— The Albigeois, Toulousain and Lauragais areas (p.49)

— The Ariege area (p.65)

— Quercorb, Corbières and Razès (p.79)

— Carcassès, Cabardès, Minervois, Béziers and Narbonne (p.107)

Itineraries follow the most direct or the most spectacular routes.

The numbers under the names of sites correspond to the pages on which the places (or their characteristic elements) are described or shown.

Key	Valleys	- - - - Départements boundaries	Main roads

1165 — Conference of Lombers

1167 — Cathar Synod of Saint-Félix-de-Caraman

1208 — Assassination of the Pope's lagate, Pierre de Castelnau, near Saint-Gilles

1209 — Innocent III's call for the crusade against the Albigeois

1209 — Sacking of Béziers

1209 — Fall of Carcassonne – Simon de Montfort is designated leader of the crusade – Death of Trencavel

1210 — Fall of Minerve, Termes and Puivert

1211 — Fall of Cabaret

1211 — Siege and burnings at Lavaur

1211 — First siege of Toulouse

1211 — Battle of Castelnaudary

1213 — Battle of Muret / Death of Pierre II of Aragon

1215 — Fourth Synod of Latran

1217 — Return of Raymond VI to Toulouse / Beginning of the second siege of Toulouse

1218 — Death of Simon de Montfort at the siege of Toulouse

1219 — Crusade of Prince Louis – Sacking of Marmande – Third siege of Toulouse

1222 — Death of Raymond VI / Raymond VII succeeds him

1223 — Death of Philippe Auguste / Louis VIII succeeds him

1224 — Armistice of Carcassonne

1226 — Royal crusade of Louis VIII / Death of Louis VIII / Regency of Blanche de Castille

1229 — Treaty of Meaux – Synod of Toulouse

1233 — Inquisition Tribunal under the responsibility of the preaching Friars

1240 — Return of Trencavel / Fall of Peyrepertuse

1244 — Surrender and burning at Montségur

1249 — Death of Raymond VII

1255 — Fall of Quéribus

1271 — Languedoc part of the kingdom of France

1321 — Burning at the stake of Bélibaste at Villerouge-Termenès

1

HISTORY

RELIGION
AND
THE CATHAR
TRAGEDY

THE COUNTRY AND ITS DESTINY

The boundary of Cathar Country is defined by the area in which the Cathar heresy spread. It started in the Albi area and the Lauragais, but its existence was felt towards the Minervois area and the Corbières, the Razès and Quercorb areas, the Ariege mountains and the Plantaurel, the Toulouse and Agen areas, and as far as the Perigord, the Quercy and the Rouergue.

A vast crescent of low fertile lands surrounded by the folds of the Pyrenean mountains to the south and by the first foothills of the Massif Central to the north, Cathar Country is congregated around a magnificent passage, the lower Aude Valley, which continues to the west with the Ariege Valley and the central Garonne Valley. Man has always understood the value of this corridor which borders the Alaric Mountain and the Black Mountain, opening onto the two great plains of the Lower Languedoc and Aquitaine. It was chosen for the building of Roman roads, postal routes, a canal, roads and motorways. All these had to cross the Naurouze Sill, a necessary crossing in the middle of the Lauragais which, despite its modest height of 300 metres above sea level, made up one of the great obstacles to be overcome during the building of Riquet's Canal of the Two Seas.

On each side of this passage, villages, towns, landscapes, fortresses perched on high and abbeys recall the crusade against the Albigensians. Even if these remains are mainly no longer what they were in the 12th and 13th centuries, they have conserved all their atmosphere and continue to fascinate. To take the time to contemplate them is to make an important step towards understanding the events which created the historic identity of the Cathar Country.

Food from the land

Whilst rich in history and landscape, the Cathar Country also possesses gastronomic riches which can only be briefly described here. Of course, it is impossible to choose between the *cassoulet* of Toulouse and that of Castelnaudary or Carcassonne! For each of them soft white haricot beans and Toulouse sausage chopped by hand are the two main ingredients of the cassole. And wine? Red wines with constancy, coming from the Carignan, Grenache Noir, Terret Noir, Cinsaut and Clairette grapes, the Corbières wines have the VDQS certificate of approval. The nine villages of Corbières, Tuchan, Paziols, Villeneuve-les-Corbières, Cascastel-des-Corbières, Fitou, Treilles, Caves, Leucate and Lapalme obtained the famous *appellation contrôlée* status in 1985.

Lézignan, the Museum of Wine: a liqueur-cabinet

nea er uolotate uiri · ſ er deo
nati ſ̄ · Et ūbū caro factū eſt ·
Et abitauit ī nobiſ · Uidimuſ
glā eiuſ · glā ꝗſi uni geniti a ꝑ
atre · Plenū gracie ⁊ ueritatiſ ·
Johs̄ teſtimoīū ꝑhibet de ipo · e
t clamabat dicenſ · hic eſt ā̄ī
diri · ꝗ poſt me uēturuſ eſt · ā̄
teme factuſ eſt · ꝗ pōr me erat ·
erat · Et de pleni tudīe eiuſ n
os oēſ acce pimuſ gr̄am ⁊ gl̄am · ꝗa
lex per moiſen data eſt · gr̄a ⁊
ueritaſ per ihm̄ xp̄m facta eſt ·

Oſ eni
ueꝰtur
ōnauit
du · ed
nār u
or · ede
nār la
ꝝeſ na
mit · de
ſc̄ā glı̄a ꝑreceb buiſ · exdo · e
ꝛenedēſia · dtuit h nr̄ī ꝝecar ti
ꝶauem tait medıſ · nꝝeſſat · ui
obrat ōl nr̄e naiſſemit ⁊r ti ua

oıa · echrem ı̄ſa adu · ꝛauioſ qu
noſ ꝑꝗuetꝫ ꝗ noſ loꝶire · ſ̄
d ı̄ſa āuoſ ꝝdo ·

Adorem deū emaniſet̄e tu
lumē ꝝecat · elaſ nr̄aſ me
utaſ greuſ oſenſioſ · Ater ga
danī ōl ꝑatre edī tiī · edī onorā
ſ̄ · etꝑir · edī onoratꝫ ſambꝰ au
āgeliſ · edī onoratꝫ ſ̄ · aꝯtoꝉi
P la oꝛō · exꝑlate · exꝑla ſaluatiō ·
tuit liditerſ glioſſeſ erehaſ ·
ōl ꝶonauratꝫ durmitꝫ āceioꝛ ·

deꝉ ſieſ enauiuo eſtār · edīnā
uoꝛ · ſ̄ · ſenlıo āuoſ ꝝduieꝛ ror g
ēā noſ ꝝeaı̄m · ꝶndicite ꝛarcꝛeꝯ ō

Q uar moutꝫ coleſ nr̄eſ ꝝe
catꝫ elt āl̄ noſ oꝛede an̄
cadıa · puuit eꝝerdia · ꝑaiau
la · ꝛeōbıa eꝛeĝō colſiueſ · abuo
lōtar eſeneſ uolōtar · Exꝶ ꝑ
la nr̄a uolōtar · iacl̄ ōnār nor
aꝝꝛetā leſ maliſtıī eꝝpırꝫ en
laſ cār̄ que ueſtem · ꝶndici
te ꝛarcıte nobıꝯ ·

M aı̄ aı̄ cūla ſā ꝝaruila
ōdu noꝛ eēnha eı̄ · ſ̄ · a

THE CATHAR RELIGION, A DUALIST CHRISTIANITY

Knowledge of the Cathar religion is supplied in the interrogation reports of the Inquisition or treatises which were passed to refute its doctrine. Evidence can also be found in apocryphal writings such as the *Interrogatio Johannis* or *The Vision of Isaiah*, in theological treatises such as *The book of the two principles* or even in rituals which contain liturgical aspects and sacraments from Catharism. It must, finally, be based on the Gospels, which make up the permanent point of reference.

In fact Catharism is a dualist Christianity. Confronted with the Roman Church, which, according to them had lost its way, (they called it the Church of Wolves) the Cathars thought that they embodied the true Church of God. They considered that there had been two creations, that of Good, work of God, and that of Evil, Emptiness, the visible world and time. These two creations, these two principles, came together in man, his eternal soul being held in the carnal prison which was the body. Christ did not appear on earth to redeem original sin but to show men the way of deliverance which would allow souls which had gone astray through the principles of Evil to come back to the kingdom of God. This way was to be baptised by the Holy Spirit, the only sacrament practised by the Cathars, that Jesus gave to the apostles. The Cathars had a single prayer, the Lord's Prayer. They rejected the Eucharist and the Cross, expression and symbol of a "conjectured" ordeal; they also refused the principle of free will, man cannot choose between Good and Evil and so, all souls created in a finite number are one day called to the eternal reckoning: they did not accept the idea of a last judgement and an eternal Hell. In order to reach the "celestial land", a soul had to be pure, and so delivered of Evil through baptism. If it had not been, or

not sufficiently, it was reincarnated in a new "skin". For the Cathars, true sins were those affecting the soul; those that Christ condemned in the Sermon on the Mount: murder, adultery, theft, swearing and blasphemy. Without supreme authority, the Cathar Church had a flexible structure; it was composed of bishoprics, in fact geographical areas, each directed by a bishop who was aided by a senior Son, his designated successor, and a minor Son who aided the senior Son. The bishop was a *parfait* among other *parfaits*, chosen by his peers. The parfait or Good Christian had received baptism, *consolamentum*, and through this had promised not to fall into temptation. He thus became a clergyman of the Cathar Church and could, in turn, dispense *consolamentum*. The Good Christian had also taken the vows of a monastic order: he refused to eat any food of animal origin, except fish, made fasts and renounced any sexual activity. He also devoted himself to living in a community and so travelled accompanied by his *socius*, another *parfait*. He also had to work: and did so in the workshops which could be found in all Cathar houses. There were women *parfaits*. They were more sedentary, in houses where young girls were brought up and single women took shelter. The faithful was composed of believers, secular people with faith and looking to come closer to the pure life of the *parfaits*. They were still subject to the principle of Evil and susceptible to sin. They would receive at their death the *consolamentum of the dying*. This ritual allowed those who participated to have a *good end*, i.e. for their soul to be reincarnated in another "skin" which was more apt to offer them a new chance of salvation. Here it must be said that while acts of the flesh were also condemned by the Cathar rule both within marriage and outside it, and if it was a mortal sin for the *parfaits*, it had the advantage of being subject to the principle of Evil when committed by the simple believer, who thus had mitigating circumstances and, in any case, it was a necessary evil, bringing reincarnation for seeking souls. Believers listened to the preaching of the *parfaits* and gave them marks of respect by practising *melioramentum*; they bowed to the ground three times while asking to be blessed. Meals were often shared by *parfaits* and believers. On these occasions, the bread was blessed by the Good Men and, the symbol of spiritual food, this *supersubstantial* bread was shared. Another Cathar rite was *aparelhament*, public confession, to which Cathar communities adhered. The *kiss of peace* concluded the ceremony. It was exchanged between *parfaits* and believers and underlined the community spirit of the assembly. We must also define what Catharism was not. It is not clear whether it was developed from Bogomilism. However,

exchanges between Cathars and Bogomils have been documented and the two doctrines, which had their roots in the same sources, were close if not identical, with the same faint differences between part dualism and absolute dualism. Most Bogomil churches, except the one in Dragovistica claimed to adhere to the first, Cathar churches in the Oc the second and those of Italy, respectively *garatenses* and *albanenses*, being divided between the two. Catharism was not a Manichean doctrine either in that its followers never referred to Manès or his writings, which were nevertheless well-known and many in number. Naturally, few material remains survive today of this religion, which was so disdainful of the world which it felt was beneath it. No churches, no statues, no frescoes, no liturgical objects. Only a few symbols, far rarer than is generally thought, which are difficult to interpret, mark the place where it took root before being hunted out and persecuted.

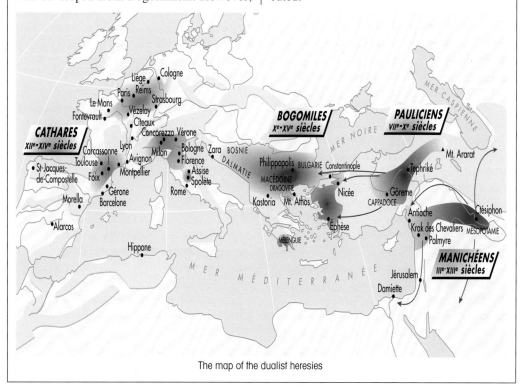

The map of the dualist heresies

The time of the heresies

As early as the first centuries of its existence, the Church was faced with the emergence of many heretical theses, particularly in Asia Minor. Some heresies in the 3rd, 4th and 5th centuries, such as Adoptianism, Arianism, Nestorianism or Monophysicism, all duly condemned by synods and councils, differed from the orthodox view on the divine nature of Christ. Others, dualist in essence, affirmed the existence of two principles, that of Good and that of Evil. In the first century, the Gnostics, who claimed their knowledge came from revelation, were the first dualists of the Christian era. Then came Marcion, also a Gnostic, who originated from the banks of the Black Sea; he was excommunicated in 144. However it was Manès, in the 3rd century in Mesopotamia, who was inspired by some precepts of Zarathustra to develop a dualist conception of the world. He and his twelve disciples spread his word from China to Egypt and from India to Arabia. In the 4th century, North Africa was reached and Augustine, before becoming the Bishop of Hippo and adversary of the Donatist and Pelagianist heresies, and later the great thinker of Christianity, was a Manichean *listener* for nine years in Carthage. Paulicianism also took some Manichean elements to appear in the 7th century in Armenia. Located in farming areas, it stirred up social discontent. The Paulician movement became of such size that

Paleochristian cross, Sbeïtla museum, Tunisia

Saint Augustine

in the beginning of the 8th century the Byzantine emperors persecuted these heretics after having tolerated them and following the re-establishing of icon worship, in 843 undertook to exterminate them. Paulicians did not hesitate to take up arms and then retreated to the east of Anatolia in Tephriké. Defeated in 872, some were deported to Thrace in the region now called Plovdiv. The Bogomil heresy started in the 10th century in Bulgaria, a region where some Paulician and Massalian elements remain (other dualists). It also has its roots in a social movement but its link with the other heresies is not established. The Bogomils, who took the name of a Macedonian priest, meaning friend of God, as the origin of the heresy, spread through a large part of the Balkans and then into Asia Minor, in Bosnia, Croatia and went on to Thrace and Southern Mesopotamia, despite the persecutions until the 14th century and in Bosnia until the Ottoman invasion in the 15th century.

THE CATHAR TRAGEDY

Occitania in the 12th century

At the end of the 12th century, the lands of the Oc language were held by princes whose power grew stronger against the Capetians who were very busy resolving conflicts with their powerful neighbours from the North, England and the Germanic Empire which only came to an end after the victory of Philip Augustus at Bouvines in 1214. These lands were shared among the Plantagenets who held Aquitaine, and these lords of the Midi: the King of Aragon, the Trencavels, Viscounts of Béziers and Carcassonne and the Counts of Toulouse. The crown of Aragon controlled the Pyrenees, Aragon, Catalonia, a part of Provence from 1168 and Roussillon as early as 1172; it had received homages from Bigorre and the Béarn and Peter II of Aragon, by marrying Marie of Montpellier in 1204, became Lord of Montpellier. After 1061, the lands of the Trencavels included the three viscounties of Béziers, Agde and Nîmes and the two counties of Carcassonne and Razès; they were surrounded by the lands of their powerful neighbours, Aragon and the Raymonds of Saint-Gilles. This particular geographical situation linked to a marked cultural connection – their lands corresponded in effect to the former Visigoth Septimania – explains the versatile nature of the diplomatic game of the Trencavels who, from 1070 to 1140 were allies of Toulouse against Barcelona, and then from 1140 were with Barcelona against Toulouse. At the end of the 12th century the situation was quite confused because even if the Trencavels gave homage to the King of Aragon they were no less vassals of the powerful and prestigious house of Toulouse, Roger Trencavel having married Azalaïs, daughter of

The dynasty of Saint-Gilles

In 840, Pepin II gave the title of Count of Toulouse to Frédelon, Count of Rouergue. In 845, Charles the Bald confirmed this title and made his brother, Raymond, Count of Quercy. When Charles the Bald, by the capitulary of Quierzy-sur-Oise authorized his vassals to hand down their privileges if they died during the expedition that he was organizing to be crowned Emperor in Rome in 877, he laid the foundations of the feudal system. It was therefore in total independence that in the early 10th century the County of Toulouse was held by Eudes, son of Raymond. The grandson of this Raymond, Raymond III Pons, annexed Septimania and extended his suzerainty to the Quercy, Albi area and the Rouergue. In the early 11th century, Guillaume Taillefer married the daughter of the Count of Arles. Thus the counts of Toulouse became marquises of Provence and increased their fiefdom with land situated north of the Durance river and the region of Beaucaire where the town of Saint-Gilles can be found, giving its name to the dynasty. Raymond IV, when he succeeded his brother Guillaume in 1088, was at the head of a kingdom. This hero of the first crusade died in 1105 in the siege of Tripoli. His wife, Elvira de Castille, gave birth to Alphonse-Jourdain in the Holy Land. The son of the latter, Raymond V, extended his suzerainty over the viscounty of Béziers and the county of Carcassonne, fiefdom of the Trencavels in 1163. Raymond VI received the Agenais area by marrying the sister of Richard the Lionheart and with his son, Raymond VII, who died in 1249, the dynasty of Saint-Gilles was no more.

Raymond V of Toulouse, in 1171. As for the Saint-Gilles family, they reigned over a vast territory which extended from the Agenais to the Marquisate of Provence and also included the Duchy of Narbonne, the County of Foix, the Quercy, the Toulouse area, the Rouergue and the Vivarais. The Count of Toulouse was a vassal of the King of France for some of his possessions, vassal to the Holy Empire for others and even vassal to the Pope for the County of Melgueil, near Montpellier. Beyond this criss-crossing of fiefdoms and vassalage, the lands of the South were united because an original Occitan culture flowered there. The singers were the troubadours who sang *fin' amors*, courtly love and celebrated *paratge*, equality in matters of the heart. Power was shared in towns between the feudal authority and the municipal institutions with respected privileges. In Toulouse as early as 1152, there was a common council whose town councillors, or *capitouls* from 1220, would obtain the recognition of "all their rights, customs and franchises" in 1189. In the *castra*, small towns, sometimes fortified, always located in strategic places, power was also shared, as well as property, between descendants: this joint-possession which excluded autocratic feudalism, also favoured dialogue within the community. From an economic point of view, money took an increasingly important part in matters; Cahors was a reputed financial centre which had struck coins since the 12th century and the name of Cahorsin was often given to those in finance; the first bill of exchange was drawn in Marseilles in 1200 and the Mills of Toulouse was a company with shares. However this atmosphere of *cortesia*, of dialogue, and this prosperity was disturbed by bands of mercenary soldiers, peasants without resources, employed by the princes. These *basques* or other *aragonais*, as they were called, meant that a climate of insecurity reigned over the lands of Oc where Catharism was to take root.

Castrum

In the lands of the Midi, the medieval town, founded in Roman times, was transformed into a walled city dominated by the *castellum*, the castle residence of the count or viscount. It was the see of a bishopric. The archetypal town is Toulouse where, as early as the 12th century, political power was shared between the lord and councillors who were responsible for the management of urban affairs. Other castles, true fortified castles such as Usson, Quéribus or Puilaurens, were purely for defensive purposes, protecting the lord and his garrison. Beyond the great city, the fortified castle and the hamlet in the clearing, was the *castrum*. Established on high ground, an obviously strategic position, the *castrum* was a number of houses grouped around a sturdy keep which, together with their thick walls and with no windows on the outer side, contributed to the protection of the site. In the *castrum* power was not held by a single lord but was shared in equal parts by the heirs, co-owners who managed the family heritage together. Thus a certain solidarity was established among the co-owners and the inhabitants, noblemen, craftsmen, doctors and peasantry and made the *castra* melting-pots where common decisions were made after long deliberations, discussions and chatter, closely linked to this Occitan culture founded on *cortesia*. These *castra* were, like Fanjeaux or Le Mas-Saintes-Puelles, ideal for the spread of the Cathar heresy and of which Simon de Montfort was justly wary as they represented considerable resistance to his quest for power. Thus in 1212 he included in the articles of the charter of Pamiers an obligation to destroy fortified churches.

1

2

The rise of Catharism

In the West, during the first millennium, heretical activity was uncommon. Of course, in the 4th century Arianism became established, fought against by the Emperor Constantine, and of course Priscillian, bishop of Lusitania, accused of Manichaeism, had been condemned by the council of Saragossa in 380 and executed in 385. However it was only half a century after Bogomilism had exploded in Bulgaria that those who were called the heretics of the year 1000 made their appearance in the West. Robert the Pious condemned ten canons to the pyre in Orléans in 1022 for their Manichaeism. It was indeed useful for the orthodox church to place its enemies within a scale of values which were already known and practised. In the same way, others were accused of being *Arians*. Almost simultaneously heretical movements appeared in Toulouse, in the Champagne area, in Arras and in Monteforte near Milan. From the mid 11th century, Gregorian reforms would bring satisfactory answers to the problems of the faithful and the development of the heresy was halted. However, in the early 12th century, while Alexis I Comnène, in Constantinople was persecuting Bogomils, the heresy took hold in Western Europe. Evangelists like Pierre de Bruys, Henri de Lausanne and Arnaud de Brescia were splitting from the orthodox church. Their actions heralded that of Pierre Valdès, the merchant from Lyon who, in 1170, sold all his worldly goods in order to follow the evangelical way of life. His 'poor of Lyon' were excommunicated in 1184 at the council of Verona. Between times, pyres were built in Cologne, in 1143 and in Liège in 1144. Also in Cologne, in 1163, five heretics were burnt and Eckbert of Schönau, canon of the cathedral, wrote: "These heretics do not hesitate to call themselves *Katharos*, that is Pure Ones". The adversary was named. As early as the beginning of the 11th century, in Champagne, near Mount Aimé, a Cathar church developed. Its members were called publicans, and it had a tragic end in 1239 since 183 of these perished on a pyre. Many Cathars, who were called *bougres* or blackguards, were arrested in Arras in 1183 and 1184. Burgundy also had its heretics, in Vézelay, Nevers, Auxerre and La Charité-sur-Loire, and its martyrs. The Italian Cathars, *patarins*, organized themselves in the churches of Concorezzo, near Milan, Desenzano, near Lake Garda, and Vicenza, Mantua, Florence and Spoleto. However it was certainly in the Languedoc where Catharism best penetrated the social fabric. Of course, here as elsewhere, the region was a cross-roads for commercial and financial exchanges and the bourgeoisie, who controlled this flow, appreciated in Catharism the recognition, as a value, of work and its acceptance of the principle of interest in money-lending. In Languedoc, however, Catharism was also able to appeal to the noblemen, whether humble or great. And this, at once for cultural reasons: Cathar communities, like those with *castra*, were places of exchanges and discussion; and in the châteaux with *fin' amors*, and in Catharism, women found their place and role. Also for other, less important reasons: Cathars did not ask these lords for money as they did not encourage them to pay a tithe to the Church, the principle of which had never been accepted in this area. But also, and perhaps above all, after having conquered the elite, the Cathars won the heart of the people who appreciated lack of riches among the ecclesiastics, admired their exemplary life and understood their teachings which were given in common language. In this Cathar Country, of course, not everyone was a heretic, and in Toulouse, the number of believers never exceeded one in ten. However the population of villages like Fanjeaux was largely converted to the heresy and, in any case, the presence of this different religion was accepted as is proved by the fact that no pyres were made in Occitania before 1209.

From anathema to the crusades

Faced with the heresy, the Catholic church re-acted with councils and preaching. In 1022, the Council of Orléans was a trial with expeditious consequences. Six councils, between 1028 and 1080, called a certain Bérenger, suspected of heresy. The Council of Toulouse in 1119 con-demned Pierre de Bruys. In Pisa in 1135, Henri de Lausanne was condemned after preaching in Le Mans and taking his heretic speeches to the region of Toulouse which led to Bernard de Clairvaux going there in 1145. In 1148 the council of Reims excommunicated the heretics and condemned Henri to prison for life. One of the canons from another council in Reims in 1157 opposed the "piffres", one of the names then given to the Cathars, called in Latin *tex-tores* or weavers, a profession which was famil-iar to them. In 1163 the council of Tours di-rected the princes to deal severely with the Cathars by imprisonment and confiscating their possessions. In the same year, Hildegarde de Bingen made a premonitory speech in Cologne: "The princes and others are going to throw themselves at the heretics and will kill them like enraged wolves...".

In Occitania, in Lombers, near Albi, in 1165, there was still time for talking and debate. A conference at which Raymond Trencavel and the Countess of Toulouse were present, op-posed Cathars, from then on called Albigen-sians, and an assembly of prelates who were di-rected by the bishop of Lodève. He concluded the debate by saying: "I consider that those who call themselves Good Men are heretics." The heresy progressed and organized itself at the Cathar council in Saint-Félix-de-Caraman in 1167 in the presence of Nicétas, a Bogomil bishop and Marcus, a representative of the Lombard community. This council defined the geographical span of the Bishoprics of Age-nais, Toulouse, Albigeios and Carcassès. In 1177, Trencavel kept the Catholic Bishop of Albi prisoner while Raymond V sent a letter to

Bernard de Clairvaux

I t was in 1112 that Bernard de Fontaine entered as a novice in the abbey of Cîteaux before becoming in 1115 the abbot of Clairvaux. In two sermons from his work the *Canticle of canticles,* he gives a contradiction to the heretic theses and in 1145 in a letter that he sent to Alphonse-Jourdain, Count of Toulouse, he asked him to intervene in order to put an end to the heretical preachings of Henri de Lausanne in the region of Toulouse. He himself undertook a trip which took him from Bordeaux to Albi via Poitiers, Périgueux, Sarlat, Tulle, Cahors and Toulouse where, at Saint-Sernin, a public discussion was organized between Bernard, Henri and the heretics who were seen as Arians. Bernard then went to Verfeil, to the east of Toulouse, that the biographer of the abbot of Clairvaux does not hesitate to call *sedes Satanae.* Bernard could not address the inhabitants who made such a disturbance that his speech went unheard. So he who would become Saint Bernard was said to have left the *castrum* hoping "that God would wither Verfeil!" a clever play on words, *verfeil* meaning *verte feuille* or green leaf in Latin.

Saint Bernard

the chapter of Cîteaux, "This pestilential contagion of heresy is so widespread that it has thrown discord among those who were united… As for me, I recognize that I do not have enough strength to bring to fruition such a vast and difficult affair, because the noblest of my land are already infected with the sickness of infidelity bringing with them a multitude of people who have abandoned the faith..." In response, a legation led by Peter of Pavia, cardinal of Saint-Chrysogone, accompanied by Henri de Marcy, abbot of Clairvaux, came to Toulouse in 1178. Pierre Maurand, a Cathar, an old and rich man was made to recant there. The legation then went on to Castres to notify Viscountess Azalaïs that Viscount Trencavel had been excommunicated for the Albi affair. The council of Latran decided in 1179 to call upon the secular power and thus marked the beginning of repression in Occitan lands. Henri de Marcy, who had become cardinal of Albano, came back to the Lauragais in 1181 at the head of a small force to lay siege to Lavaur and to take charge, from Azalaïs, of two Cathars including the bishop of the Church of Toulouse, who recanted. During nearly twenty years, doctrinal quarrels seemed to subside even if the decree of Verona in 1184 whipped up all the heretics once again and invited all local clergymen to hunt them down. However it was the first years of Pope Innocent III which marked the start of a systematic fight against Catharism. It is true that the young pope – he was thirty-eight years old when he was elected in 1198 –, a lawyer beyond comparison – he had been taught at Bologna University –, found himself faced, upon taking office, with very serious external problems: Jerusalem had been taken by the Moslems in 1187 and the Castillians had been defeated by other Moslems in Spain at the battle of Alarcos in 1195. After a call addressed to the archbishop of Auch and faced with his weak co-operation, and, in general, that of the local clergy, he quickly sent legates to the Languedoc and signed the decree of Viterbe in 1199 which legally confirmed the

Castres: old houses on the Agout river

principle of dispossession of those guilty of heresy. The first legate was his confessor, Rainier, seconded by Pierre de Castelnau, archdeacon of Maguelone who, in 1203, headed the legation. He was then a monk at the Abbey of Fontfroide from where another monk, Brother Raoul, accompanied him. The two legates went first to Toulouse where they negotiated their own commitment to respect the customs and privileges of the town, and that of the inhabitants to "keep the Roman Catholic faith". In Aragon, the pope was able to count on Peter II, the Christian king who had condemned the heretics of his kingdom to death in Gerona in 1198. In 1204, the king of Aragon seemed to alter his position. He organized a conference between Cathars, Vaudois and Catholics in Carcassonne in the presence of the legates and the Cathar bishop of Carcassès and signed a pact of mutual assistance in Millau with Raymond VI, his brother-in-law, who had always adopted, contrarily to his father who he had succeeded in 1194, a tolerant attitude to the

The Vaudois

Around 1175, Pierre Valdès, a Lyon merchant, had the Gospels translated into Provençal and distributed his riches to the poor. He then led an itinerant life and preached for a return to evangelical purity. His doctrine was condemned at the Council of Latran in 1179 and in 1184 the Vaudois were excommunicated, like the Cathars at the Council of Verona. In the early 13th century, some Vaudois were reconciled with the church, while the others were persecuted: eighty were burnt in 1211 in Strasbourg. The poor of Lyon hid in the Lubéron and the Alps. In 1390, 120 of them died on the pyre near Freissinières and in 1487, Albert de Catane called for a crusade against the Vaudois of which the last few took refuge in Dormillouse, called the "Montségur of the poor" before being exterminated.

heretics. Pope Innocent III then reinforced the presence of the Cistercians as a solution to the *negotium pacis et fidei*, the Albigensian crisis, by naming Arnaud-Amaury, abbot of Citeaux in person to head his legation, and twice invited, in vain, Philip Augustus to intervene in the Midi in 1204 and 1205. In 1206 six hundred Cathars participated in a council in Mirepoix and demanded that Raymond de Péreille re-establish the defences at Monségur Castle. It was in the same year that the bishop of Osma, Diègue, and his sub-prior Dominic, met the papal legates in Montpellier who were somewhat discouraged. He advised them to fight heresy on its own ground by renouncing any outward signs of wealth and sending their retinue back to Spain, decided to accompany them in their apostolic travels. The group moved on foot, living from begging. In Servian, Béziers and Verfeil he obtained encouraging results from his preachings and in the following year founded a convent of nuns in the heart of Cathar Country in Prouille in the Lauragais. In 1207, relations between Pope Innocent III and Raymond VI deteriorated. The pope excommunicated the count, reproaching him for his use of mercenaries, non-respect of the peace of God, the expulsion of the bishop of Carpentras and the protection of the heretics on his lands that he threatened to "expose as prey"; he once again demanded, but with no more success, that the king of France should intervene. Feeling the danger, the Count of Toulouse called on Pierre de Castelnau in January 1208 at Saint-Gilles near the Little Rhône in order to reconcile himself with the Church. The turbulent meeting finished in failure. On 14 January while he was preparing to cross the Rhône, probably near Arles, the legate was assassinated. Raymond VI was suspected of instigating the murder. Pope Innocent III then made a call for a crusade against the Cathars, the only crusade ever led on Catholic lands, thus fulfilling the terrible prophesy of Dominic, "... where blessing has no value, the stick will be used...".

The crusade against the Albigensians

Arnaud-Amaury, abbot of Cîteaux was responsible for raising the company of crusaders. Philip Augustus refused to participate in the crusade but authorized some of his vassals to do so. Raymond VI multiplied the number of diplomatic initiatives. He met Arnaud-Amaury in Aubenas and sent, at the end of 1208, an ambassador to Rome, the archbishop of Auch. At the same time he suggested to Trencavel, who refused, to form a united front. He was finally called to Valence by the legate Milon, in June 1209. He had to give seven of his fortresses as security and make a full apology in Saint-Gilles on 18 June 1209. He swore to fight the heretics and cleverly, asked to take the cross, thus putting even his land under the protection of the Pope. Raymond-Roger Trencavel, the Viscount of Béziers and Carcassonnne, wanted to do the same but the pope refused. The ost, the army of crusaders, was powerful. The pardon of sins committed, the proximity of battlefields and land there for the taking were certainly attractions for more than one lord. Most of the group left Lyon on 24 June 1209 and travelled along the Rhône Valley. Two other groups were formed; one, led by the archbishop of Bordeaux and the Count of the Auvergne travelled in the Quercy and Agen areas where they sacked Tonneins. Another group led by the bishop of Le Puy joined them in Casseneil where the first pyre of the crusade was lit. On 21 July 1209, Arnaud-Amaury and the crusaders arrived at Béziers. The inhabitants refused to give themselves up and surrender the Cathars. The town was sacked. The crusaders obtained the submission and support of the town of Narbonne who gave them Viscount Aimery and Archbishop Bérenger as well as those of Montpellier and Arles. Then the ost went on to Carcassonne where Trencavel had entrenched himself. They arrived under the ramparts in early August. The siege was held in the hot summer sun and

Kill them all...

It was on 21 July 1209 that the army of crusaders arrived at Béziers. The town, clustered around its cathedral, rose above the Orb river. Viscount Raymond-Roger Trencavel was absent, having gone to organize the defence of Carcassonne. The inhabitants of Béziers bravely refused the offer of the crusaders to deliver up the Cathars "so as not to share their fate nor to die with them". A long siege seemed to be ahead but the next day a group of those besieged tried a possibly unwise escape. They were pursued by a band of soldiers who succeeded in entering the town. The crusaders set fire to and massacred nearly all the population, almost twenty thousand people, even the seven thousand of them who had taken refuge in the Church of the Magdalene. Pierre des Vaux-de-Cernay noted that the 22 July was the day of Saint Magdalene and that, as fate would have it, it was in that same church that in 1167 Viscount Raymond Trencavel had been assassinated by the Biterrois who broke the teeth of the bishop who had taken his side. Faced with the hesitation of some crusades to commit such horrific acts, Arnaud-Amaury, abbot of Cîteaux and spiritual leader of the crusade is truly said to have cried: "Kill them all! God will recognize his own!" In any case, this little phrase was reported ten years later by Césaire de Heisterbach, a Cistercian monk from Cologne. And the terrible warnings of Guillaume de Tudèle, the author of the song of the crusades against the Albigensians rang out: "Any castle which resists, any stubborn town shall be taken by force and reduced to a charnel-house. That no living being should be left, even new-born babies. Thus shall be sown healthy fear and no longer shall anyone dare to defy the Cross of God..."

the crusaders became masters of sources of water. After an unsuccessful attempt to mediate by his suzerain, Peter II of Aragon, Trencavel, obliged to negotiate, was taken prisoner. His surrender is an enigma. He had come to parley and found himself in a deep dungeon where he died of dysentery for some, poisoned for others on 10 November 1209. Carcassonne was held, and its terrified inhabitants ran away. In the crusaders' camp, Raymond VI had been a spectator to the fall of Trencavel. Arnaud-Amaury wanted to give the fiefdom of the Trencavels to a crusading lord. Many declined the offer. The service of ost was only forty days and moreover they did not want to dispossess another lord even if he was accused of heresy. One of them finally accepted and at the same time became head of the crusade. He came from Île-de-France and his name was Simon de Montfort.

He had to subdue the lands that he had received. The task was difficult as he only had around thirty knights at his side, the others having left as their ost service was over. During the autumn of 1209, he was in Alzonne, Montréal, Fanjeaux where he met his brother Dominic, Limoux and Preixan where he made peace with the Count of Foix. Castres – where two Cathars died on a pyre – submitted but the first siege of the castles of Cabaret, Surdespine and Quertinheux failed. Montfort then occupied Mirepoix, although the lord Pierre-Roger was a convinced Cathar, and Pamiers, before going to Lombers and Albi. In late September 1209, Raymond-Roger of Foix took back Preixan and tried unsuccessfully to take Fanjeaux. In November in Montpellier, Agnès, Trencavel's widow – he had just died – gave away all her rights to Montfort who had in fact offered his homage to Peter II of Aragon, the legitimate sovereign of the Viscounty of Carcassonne. The latter however, refused. Revolt rumbled in the conquered lands, Castres and Lombers particularly rose up. Montfort lost many localities but had to wait to receive reinforcements, led by his wife, Alix de

Song, history and chronicle

The Western Crusades and those in the Iberian peninsula had had their songs, epic poems which chronicled them. With *La Canso* the crusade against the Albigensians had its own. "In verses of the same sort and to the same music" as the *Canso d'Antiocha*, composed in Occitan verse in the 1130s by Gregori Bechada of Limoges, the work relates the events from 1209 to 1218. In fact it had two parts, each of them being the work of a different author. The first part with 2749 verses making 130 tirades, covered the period from 1209 to the eve of the battle of Muret in 1213. Guillaume de Tudèle, a scholar from Navarre and a member of the retinue of Baudouin, the brother of Raymond VI who had gone overto the crusaders' camp, wrote it in Occitan which was full of gallicized expressions. In Bruniquel, in the Aveyron gorges, he took the side of the Crusaders. The second part, in 83 tirades and 6811 verses, goes from the battle of Muret to that of Baziège, where its anonymous author had certainly been present. The Occitan of this great poet, probably from Toulouse and with all his heart on the side of the people in the Midi, was very pure. Pierre des Vaux-de-Cernay left us a much less poetic work, more official in nature: *Hystoria albigensis, the Albigensian Story*. Witness to these events, he was the nephew of Guy des Vaux-de-Cernay, bishop of Carcassonne and like him, defended the crusaders' actions in the Languedoc. Guillaume de Puylaurens wrote a short chronicle in Latin in the mid-thirteenth century about the crusade and the links of the Count of Toulouse with the Capetian domain. Although close to Foulque, bishop of Toulouse, he adopted a more uncertain position than Pierre des Vaux-de-Cernay.

Montmorency, until March 1210 in Pezenas to once more take up the offensive. He inflicted an exemplary punishment on the defenders of Bram who had dared to resist him. He had a hundred prisoners mutilated – eyes torn out, nose, ears and upper lips cut off – and had them led, by the only person who had only been blinded in one eye, to the fortresses of Cabaret, still unconquered. The threat was a strong one, but Cabaret was well defended by Pierre-Roger and Jourdain de Cabaret, and did not succumb. Then Montfort turned his attentions to Minerve. He had the town destroyed with his war machines, ruining it and depriving it of water, obliging Guillaume de Minerve to give up after five weeks of siege. The crusaders invaded the fortress and on 22 July 1210 one hundred and forty Cathars preferred the pyre to recanting. Other fortresses fell. In August it was the imposing Citadel of Termes which was besieged. There was a lack of water and the town was going to give up when a violent storm refilled the stocks. People rushed to the water, which was unfortunately polluted, and dysentery obliged the besieged town to run for escape. Raymond de Termes was captured and imprisoned in a Carcassonne jail where he died in 1213. Then it was the Castle of Puivert which submitted to the leader of the crusaders. The lords of the Midi thus lost, one by one, titles and land, becoming dispossessed lords or *faidits*. The first six months of the year 1211 left Raymond VI in isolation. Indeed in January, a conference brought together first in Narbonne then in Montpellier, the papal legates, Arnaud-Amaury, Thédise, Raymond d'Uzès, the lords of the Midi and Simon de Montfort. On this occasion, Peter II guaranteed the neutrality of the Count of Foix, eventually accepted the homage of Montfort and even organized the marriage of his son Jacques to Amicie the daughter of the leader of the crusade. Raymond VI, however, disgusted by the unacceptable conditions that the legates wanted to impose on him, refused and was excommunicated on 6 February and would

Raymond VI of Saint-Gilles

Raymond VI was born in 1156 and inherited the title of Count of Toulouse in 1194. Great-grandson of Raymond IV, one of the figures of the first crusade, he adopted a sometimes ambiguous attitude as he wanted to preserve the unity and integrality of the county even at the heart of unrest without equal. A Catholic, he seemed sincere when he made donations to the abbeys of his county but he was also disturbingly tolerant towards the heretics who were many on his lands and in his entourage. He was excommunicated for the double accusation of heresy and having participated in the murder of Pierre de Castelnau in 1208. Raymond VI felt very divided between his wish to remain a good Christian, obeying the Church and his inability to take up arms against his own subjects the Cathars for whom he visibly had a certain sympathy. In order to avoid a war of crusades in which he had everything to lose, he accepted, during a humiliating ceremony on the parvis of the abbey church in Saint-Gilles on 18 June 1209 to make a full apology. A lost cause since the crusade was already under way. So he took up the cross himself hoping to reduce the murderous ardour of the crusaders by his presence. However, incessantly hunted by the hatred of the legate of the pope Arnaud-Amaury and Foulque, the bishop of Toulouse, Raymond VI could only fear the effects of a religious and military expedition which wanted to wipe him out. He has been described as a coward, indecisive, even feeble. He was however none of these. He had been taught to think, to weigh his chances, to take time, to negotiate in order to succeed. He used these virtues for the best but between 1209 and 1222, the date of his death, they had no chance of being fulfilled.

remain so until his death. Montfort was able to continue his quest for power. In March he became master, without opposition, of the castles of Cabaret. Indeed Pierre-Roger de Cabaret negotiated his surrender for land in the Biterrois and gave his fortresses to his prisoner, Bouchard de Marly, Montfort's own cousin, who he had kept captive since 1209. Now Lavaur had to be taken. After a month of siege, the town was captured. Eighty knights were hung and four hundred Cathars burnt on the largest pyre of the crusade. Lady Guiraude, the chatelaine of Lavaur was thrown to the bottom of a well and buried under stones. Some days later Puylaurens was occupied and around sixty Cathars were burnt in the village of Les Cassées. In May, Baudouin, brother of Raymond VI, gave up Montferrand to Montfort. This treachery was explained by the fragile relations between the two brothers. Baudouin, badly treated as the younger brother, had never had any great enthusiasm for the Occitan cause. Raymond VI would not forgive him and had him hung in Montauban on 17 February 1214. Just before summer 1211, the crusaders were leaving on a campaign in the Rouergue, and in the Albigeois. Rabastens, Gaillac and Puycelci, and Saint-Antonin opened their gates. Bruniquel, where Raymond VI was staying, passed into the crusaders' hands and Montfort gave the castle to Baudouin. On 17 June 1211, Montfort laid siege to Toulouse for the first time, but it was a failure. After a raid on Foix, he left on a pilgrimage to Rocamadour, not without passing through Cahors, his new fiefdom – the bishop of the town, in the presence of Brother Dominic, had sworn allegiance to him at the walls of the besieged Toulouse. While Raymond VI and his vassals were raising forces in the Lauragais, Montfort entrenched himself at Castelnaudary. The battle in September 1211 was indecisive but each party claimed victory.

Montfort spent Christmas in Castres, before starting a campaign in 1212. For no place was definitively conquered. Cahuzac, Gaillac,

The battle of Castelnaudary

The battle of Castelnaudary, in September 1211, is told by Guilhem de Tudèle, in his *Canso,* in more than three hundred epic verses. The troops of Raymond VI, who had been joined by those of Raymond-Roger de Foix, Gaston de Béarn, Hugues d'Alfaro and Savary de Mauléon, arrived near Castelnaudary "covering the ground like grasshoppers", tells Pierre des Vaux-de-Cernay. The army thus formed included five thousand men. Camp was built near the castle of Castelnaudary where Montfort had entrenched himself with five hundred of his men. The conviction with which the lords of the Midi started the siege was quite relative as Pierre des Vaux-de-Cernay tells that those under siege went out for the wine harvest watched by their attackers. Montfort sent a messenger to Bouchard de Marly, who was in Lavaur, to ask for reinforcements. The latter and some other knights came through Saissac. Montfort, knowing that they would be attacked, sent forty knights to their aid when from Carcassonne Guy de Lévis came to the rescue. The Count of Foix reassembled his men and engaged in a pitched battle against these reinforcements. Montfort left the castle with the sixty knights and horsemen who had stayed with him to lend a helping hand to the faithful. The losses were slight on the French side but much heavier for the Occitans. Nevertheless, Montfort gave up on attacking their camp and went back to the castle. The lords of the Midi, realising that the siege was pointless, set fire to their weapons and broke camp. In the military sense he was neither conqueror nor conquered but Montfort had held up his head to the southern coalition which was decidedly more fragile.

②

Rabastens and Montégut fell or were taken back in March. In April and May it was the turn of Hautpoul, Puylaurens, Saint-Marcel, Laguépie and Saint-Antonin. During the summer, the crusaders also seized Penne-d'Agenais and Biron in the Périgord. The taking of Moissac, in the Quercy then occurred. After an expedition in the Ariege, Couserans and Comminges, Montfort took winter quarters in Pamiers. It was there that he wrote the charter of Pamiers which, in forty-six articles, fixed the ways and customs for the conquered lands. At the end of 1212 Montfort must have been satisfied: only Toulouse and Montauban were not yet taken. Raymond VI left for Aragon to ask for help from Peter II, his brother-in-law. The latter, victorious after the Almohades in Las Navas de Tolosa on 12 July 1212, convinced the Pope to stop the crusade but in January 1213, at the Council of Lavaur, the Falcon Party blocked the peace process. Peter II therefore spread his royal protection over the northern Pyrenean possessions of the Counts

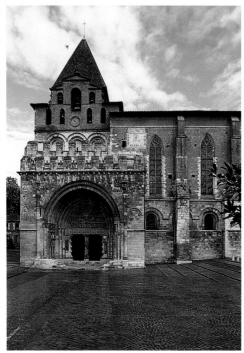

Moissac: the bell-tower porch of Saint Peter's Church

The Charter of Pamiers

In the month of November 1212, Simon de Montfort called, at Pamiers, an assembly made up of bishops and the lords of the lands under his control. This assembly named a commission of twelve members: the bishops of Toulouse and Couserans, a Templar and a Hospitaller, four knights from the North of France and four from the South, who, after having sworn an oath on the Evangelist Saints wrote the forty-six articles of the charter of Pamiers. They had to define the rights, ways and customs for the conquered lands, and dealt with the great problems brought up by the crusade: the immunity of clerics, the destruction of fortified churches and the creation of places of worship. Where there were houses of heretics, the fate of the heretics had to be decided, and a permanent army of Northern French had to be constituted and placed under the Montfort's command. They also included rules against forming leagues and associations directed against Montfort and inheritance laws taken from the customs of the North of France, and the forbidding of private vengeance. It has to be said that these laws took some liberties with feudal law since none of the articles referred to the *main lord* whether it be the king of Aragon for the viscounty of Béziers and of Carcassonne or the King of France for the other lands. Simon de Montfort acted as a true monarch, as if he had no justification to give to anyone, apart, perhaps, to the pope whose champion he had made himself. He promised in these laws to collect taxes for the pope and to bring back tithes and lift the property qualifications on all excommunicated persons. And on 1 December 1212 the laws were officially proclaimed.

of Toulouse, Comminges and Foix as well as the Viscounty of Béarn, and in this way made up a vast Mediterranean state from the Ebre to beyond the Rhône. This sovereignty implied military aid. The troops of Peter II then joined those of his vassals outside Muret which was occupied by the crusaders. On 12 September 1213, the two camps met in a battle where the Occitans were far stronger in number. However, during the fighting, Peter II met his death. It was the undoing of the Occitans. After the battle of Muret, the situation became confused. Raymond VI took refuge in England. Montfort did not occupy Toulouse although it was within his reach, but left to overcome some problems in Provence. With the threat of advances by John Lackland, who had landed in La Rochelle in February 1214, the crusaders' situation deteriorated and it took all the competency of the new papal legate, Pierre de Bénévent, to obtain, by the declarations of Narbonne in April 1214, the submission to the Church of the Counts of Foix and Comminges.

Saint-Just de Valcabrère and Saint-Bertrand-de-Comminges

The sinister rumour of disaster

On 8 September 1213, Peter II of Aragon made camp in front of the *castrum* of Muret around twenty kilometres from Toulouse. He had at his side the Counts of Comminges and Foix, his vassals. RaymondVI joined them there. Montfort was in Fanjeaux when he heard the news; he reunited the crusaders from Le Carcassès and moved on towards Muret via the Abbey of Boulbonne. Seven bishops and three abbots accompanied him who, on the orders of Arnaud-Amaury were to try to negotiate. The latter, who had been present at Las Navas de Tolosa at the side of Peter II must have been conscious of the paradox represented by a battle which opposed the crusaders to someone who, a year earlier had been the champion of Christianity. On 11 September these bishops excommunicated the Counts of Toulouse, Comminges and Foix at the famous mass celebrated in Saverdun, and the same evening entered Muret with Montfort. On the morning of 12 September with Foulque at their head, they made a last appeal to Peter II who remained inflexible. Armed confrontations were inevitable. After being blessed by the bishops the crusaders led by Montfort and divided into three squadrons left Muret. The two first squadrons took the initiative to attack and crossed the first Occitan lines. It was during these attacks that Peter II was killed. Montfort then attacked others from the Midi while those from Toulouse tried to enter Muret. However news of the death of the King of Aragon spread like wildfire through the southern ranks and led to their undoing. Many ran to the Garonne river and many died by drowning. And the Anonymous author wrote "The sinister rumour of disaster is already spreading throughout the world…"

Raymond VI who had returned to his land did the same. However Montfort, always ready, continued his search for conquests in June in the Périgord and Rouergue. The Capetian then decided to change his strategy of waiting and, in Spring 1215 Prince Louis, the son of Philip Augustus, came on a pilgrimage to the Midi. With Montfort, who went to welcome him in the Vienne, he entered Toulouse, whose defences he had destroyed. At the Council of Latran in November 1215, Raymond VI was stripped of his rights in favour of Montfort who became Count of Toulouse. The canons at this 4th ecumenical council presided over by Pope Innocent III confirmed, in fact, the anti-heretical actions of earlier local councils: the heretics saw their possessions confiscated, lost their citizenship and were declared unfit for public office. The return of the Raymonds, father and son, who landed in Marseilles in January 1216 to move on to Avignon, sowed a seed of hope in Provence and fanned the flames of Occitan patriotism. While Simon de Montfort was having his title of Count of Toulouse confirmed before Philip Augustus in Paris and Raymond VI left to raise troops in Aragon, "Raymondet" entered Beaucaire untroubled where a crusader garrison entrenched in the citadel did not wish to surrender. Simon de Montfort came back from Paris as fast as possible but stopped in Beaucaire where he learnt of the death of Innocent III. He abandoned the siege because another far more serious danger was looming. Toulouse had revolted during his absence. He rode on to Toulouse. Bishop Foulque had promised clemency for the inhabitants of Toulouse but Montfort, in the church of Saint-Pierre des Cuisines denounced the amnesty promised by the prelate and quelled these troubles with extreme severity. Montfort then went to Tarbes to establish his sovereignty over Bigorre. He married his son Guy to Pétronille, the Countess of Bigorre in November 1216 and unsuccessfully laid siege to the castle of Lourdes. In March 1217 he attacked on the lands of the Count of Foix that the latter had neverthe-

The Council of Latran

It was in the Palace of Latran, a possession of the pope, that from the first of November 1215, the 12th ecumenical council was to be held, also called Latran IV, called for by Innocent III. Nearly two thousand three hundred people arrived. The programme was very thorough and had existed as early as 1213. We must: "tear out vices and plant virtues, correct abuse and reform customs, suppress the heresies and strengthen faith, calm discord and make peace reign." It was a vast programme which Innocent III was not sure of bringing to a successful conclusion because his health faltered under such a heavy burden of responsibility. The Languedoc, at the heart of the debate had sent the protagonists of the Cathar drama: the members of the Occitan clergy with Arnaud-Amaury at their head but also Raymond VI de Toulouse and Raymond-Roger de Foix. Simon de Montfort was represented by his brother Guy. Dominic, who wanted to created an order of Preaching Brothers, the future Dominicans, came in person to defend his ideas. The debates on the crusade against the Albigensians were turbulent and tense. The Holy Father himself, disavowed by the assembly of clerics when he asked for indulgence towards the Count of Toulouse had to give way. On 14 December 1215, the sentence fell, heavy with consequences: "...Raymond, formerly Count of Toulouse is found guilty...to be forever deprived of his property rights which have been exercised too often in the cause of evil." All the land conquered by the crusaders was given to Count de Montfort. The rest was sequestered until the young Count Raymond VII could take possession. Thus the council concluded with the fall of a great prince of the West.

less given to the Church as a pledge. Montfort besieged Montgaillard and occupied the castle of Foix. In May, he re-established order in the Corbières and received the surrender of Guillaume de Peyrepertuse and then went to fight in the Rhône Valley at the side of Viviers, Montélimar and Crest. During his absence, the lords of the Midi, Raymond VI of Toulouse, Roger-Bernard de Foix and Bernard de Comminges met in Saint-Lizier in September and agreed to unite their forces against the French. Raymond VI had decided to return to his town and accompanied by his allies crossed the Garonne at Cazères. On 12 September 1217 in La Salvetat, they destroyed the small troop that Jori, the crusader lord responsible for Comminges had sent ahead. The way was then free. Raymond VI entered Toulouse over Bazacle ford on 13 September 1217 to the acclaims of the inhabitants who rushed ahead of their lord. He put the town under protection and confirmed the consulate that Simon de Montfort had tried to abolish. The latter, who had hurried back, arrived at the beginning of October in the crusaders' camp at the foot of the walls of Narbonne Castle. The second siege of Toulouse began, and lasted ten months during which the French also had to deal with an uprising in Montauban. At the end of May 1218, Raymond VI named his son Raymond the Young as his successor who entered Toulouse a few days later. During this time, murderous attacks were made but the town resisted. The challenge was great, Montfort had sworn to take Toulouse or die under its walls! Battle raged on 25 June 1218. Guy de Montfort, the brother of Simon, was struck by the arrow of a crossbow. Montfort rushed to him. A mangonel had been fixed on the top of the ramparts. It was operated by a group of women. Montfort, his skull shattered, collapsed. A chant rose up from Toulouse: "*Montfort es mort. Viva Tolosa gloriosa et poderosa. Tornan lo paratge et l'onor*". It was Amaury, son of Montfort who at twenty years old became the head of the crusade.

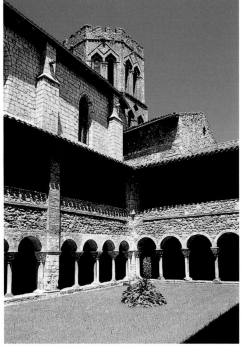
Saint-Lizier: the cathedral cloister

Toulouse: windows of the Mill of Narbonne Castle

Simon de Montfort, the Lion of the Crusade

The fortifications of Toulouse, painting by Jean-Paul Laurens

Simon de Montfort, painting by Dejuinne

Simon IV de Montfort was born around 1150. He was lord of Montfort and Épernon. In 1209, when he decided to participate in the crusade against the Albigensians, he was almost sixty years old. Pierre des Vaux-de-Cernay paints a picture of a courageous legendary knight. The two men knew each other well. They fought together in the fourth crusade and outside Zara, a Christian town, they both refused to lay siege at the side of the Venetians. With a mission in which he firmly believed, he directed for nearly nine years a relentless expedition in the southern regions. His piety was only equalled by his courage but nevertheless he has also left an image of an ambitious conqueror and a cruel warrior. So it is not surprising that the inhabitants of Toulouse sang out their joy and relief at his death in 1218. A strategically placed mangonel on the ramparts of Toulouse, operated, according to legend, by women and young girls, put an end to his days. Let us listen to Pierre des Vaux-de-Cernay: "And the stone went straight to its target and hit the count's steel helmet so hard that his eyes, brain, teeth, forehead and jaw were shattered and he fell to the ground, dead, bleeding and black." Listen to the inhabitants of Toulouse singing in their own language of Occitan: "*Viva Tolosa, ciutat gloriosa et poderosa tornan lo paratge e l'onor, Montfort es mort!*" ("Long live Toulouse, glorious and powerful city. Noblesse and honour have returned, Montfort is dead!), Gallant, courteous, brave, just or cruel, murderous, bloody… so many adjectives used by the chroniclers of the crusade against the Albigensians to try to define a personality which was certainly out of the ordinary and which well deserves the name of "Lion of the Crusade"!

Reconquest and surrender

The inheritance of Amaury de Montfort was very difficult to manage. After a last fight of the crusaders, the siege of Toulouse was lifted on 25 July 1218. Montfort was buried in Carcassonne. He was a "saint and a martyr", Foulque, the bishop of Toulouse is said to have proclaimed as a funeral elegy. For the Occitan camp in which Raymond the Young was confirming his authority, the hour for victory had come. The Count of Comminges, Bernard IV, defeated the crusaders in Meilhan; Raymond VI re-established his power in the Agenais, the Quercy, Rouergue and Lower Languedoc. In early 1219, in Baziège, at a pitched battle, the Southerners won a victory over the French. Honorius III, the pope finally persuaded Philip Augustus to send his son to the aid of the crusade. Prince Louis joined Amaury de Montfort on 3 June 1219 in Marmande which was sacked and burned, and all the inhabitants were massacred. The anonymous author of *La Canso* tells: "And the earth, the ground and the river bank were crimson with the blood which ran over them. No man, woman, child, old man or creature was left alive unless they were hidden. The town was destroyed and the fire, alight..." Louis left to besiege Toulouse but after the failure of what was to be the third siege of Toulouse, Louis, his military service accomplished, departed. In Castelnaudary in July 1220, Guy died, brother of Amaury who saw the property left by his father being crumbled away. To save it, he gave it as a donation to the King of France, who did not react; no more did he to the letter of surrender which was addressed to him in June 1222 by the future Raymond VII two months before the death of his father. Other players in this drama then disappeared: Raymond-Roger de Foix, in March 1223, after having freed Mirepoix, and Philip Augustus on 14 July. In January 1224, the armistice of Carcassonne led to the defeat of the Montforts. Amaury de Montfort took back to France the body of his father wrapped in an ox-skin for fear that his tomb in Saint Nazaire Cathedral would be desecrated. The young Trencavel, son of Raymond-Roger Trencavel who had died in the jails of Carcassonne in November 1209, came back from exile and was able to take back his fiefdom for a few years. Prince Louis had succeeded his father under the name of Louis VIII. The new king wanted to put an end to the Occitan affair. Curiously, Honorius III asked him to hold back and invited the Southerners to negotiate. In Montpellier in August 1224, Raymond VII, Trencavel and the Count of Foix promised to fight the heresy and recognized the authority of the king to Arnaud-Amaury. However, in a dramatic event, the Council of Bourges in 1225 did not keep to the Montpellier agreements: Raymond VII was dispossessed and excommunicated. He received absolution on condition that he abandoned all his lands and claim to them for ever, which was an unacceptable clause. His refusal unleashed the Royal Crusade. In 1226, Louis VIII in person led the crusade and took to the Rhône Valley. Avignon opposed him violently and only ceded after a long siege on 12 September 1226. Occitan solidarity had been somewhat cracked during the month of August under the ramparts of Avignon. Bernard V of Comminges had come but had not fought, even though his father Bernard IV had been a figurehead to southern resistance. After the surrender of Avignon, the towns of the Midi gave up when they heard of the coming of Louis' troops: the memory of Marmande was a painful one. It must be said that while the Royal Crusade was unfolding, the Cathar church remained firmly rooted in the Languedoc. Cabaret became one of their sanctuaries and at the Council of Pieusse in 1226, around Guilhabert de Castres, a hundred *parfaits* decided to create the new Cathar bishopric of Razès between that of Carcassès and the Toulouse area. Benoît de Termes who was named bishop, his senior Son was Raymond Agulher and his minor Son was Pons Bernard. However the Cathars still had to pay with their blood and during the Royal Crusade Pierre

Isarn, their bishop of Carcassonne was captured by the seneschal of Beaujeu and burnt alive in Caunes in the presence of the king. The latter was sick and renounced on attacking Toulouse directly, deciding to return to Ile-de-France via the Massif Central. He died in Montpensier on 8 November 1226 at the age of thirty-nine. His son was only six years old. He was immediately consecrated king in Reims under the name of Louis IX and it was his mother, Blanche de Castille who became regent of the kingdom for him. In the Languedoc, pockets of resistance remained, such as in Limoux where the Count of Foix and Trencavel, also excommunicated, had taken refuge. During the summer of 1227, the royal army led by Imbert de Beaujeu massacred the population of Labécède: "Gone by the sword, gone by the stake" wrote Guillaume de Puylaurens. In Castelsarrasin in May 1228, Raymond VII had a clear victory over the royal troops who, soon after, laid siege to Toulouse and destroyed the crops. Although undefeated, Raymond VII pre-

Labécède-Lauragais: the anthromorphous grave-marker

ferred to negotiate. The monarchy did everything possible to do so and rushed to Count Elie Garin, abbot of Grandselve who met Raymond VII in Baziège in December 1228. Preliminary agreements to the signing of the Treaty of Meaux between the Count of Toulouse and Blanche de Castille were made. However, in signing the treaty of Paris in April 1229, which added to that of Meaux, Raymond VII agreed to total surrender. On 25 April 1229 from the Louvre where he was practically a prisoner, he wrote to Roger-Bernard de Foix to recommend that he accept peace. It was a veritable crusading army that the Count of Foix met in Saint-Jean-de-Verges on 16 June 1229: he could only surrender. The Languedoc then entered the "Peace of the Church and the King".

Applying the Treaty of Meaux, the Cardinal of Saint-Ange called the Council of Toulouse in November 1229 which stopped the methods of repression of the heresy in practice. The foundation of the University of Theology of Toulouse, one master of which was Roland de Crémone, an eminent theologian was basically a result of this action. Raymond VII continued to pursue his objectives, to get back his possessions and titles, to ensure the continuing of his dynasty and to give a Christian grave to his father; but the religious powers, despite the participation of the count in an expedition to the Black Mountain in 1232 which resulted in the capture of nineteen *parfaits* including Pagan the Lord of Labécède, always reproached him his lack of commitment. He had to give guarantees of goodwill and to proclaim an anti-Cathar edict in Toulouse on 20 April 1233. It was in the same year that Gregory IX gave the Preaching Brothers the mission of the Inquisition which had until then been led by the bishops. The excesses of the trials led to firm and declared hostility towards him by Raymond VII and also the hostility of the populations of Albi, Narbonne, Cordes and even Toulouse. Hunted down, the heretics took refuge in Puilaurens, Peyrepertuse, Quéribus and Montségur that in 1232 had been made "the head and seat" of the Cathar

The Treaty of Meaux

In the Treaty of Meaux, Raymond VII abandoned all his possessions in the Lower Languedoc and Provence. He promised to marry Jeanne, his nine-year-old daughter to Alphonse de Poitiers, the brother of the future king Louis IX. Through the clauses of succession in the treaty the County of Toulouse would become a Capetian possession at Jeanne's death. Raymond VII also promised to fight the heresy on his lands and to make a pilgrimage to the Holy Land – which he never did. Raymond VII and the *faidits*, except the heretics, took possession once again of land which had been given to Montfort. Also Toulouse and thirty towns including Casseneuil, Avignonet, Auterive and Montauban had their fortifications destroyed. Narbonne Castle, the true counts' castle was occupied by a royal garrison. Finally, and to add insult to injury, the financial conditions which were imposed on the Count of Toulouse were exorbitant, making it impossible for him to form an army. It must be noted that the castle of Penne d'Albigeois was the object of a special clause, which explains much about the capacity to resist of some Southerners, the reputation of the lords of Penne, and the defensive qualities of the eagle's nest of the Aveyron Gorges. On Thursday 12 April 1229, a Holy Thursday, in front of the doorway of Notre Dame in the presence of the future king who was only fifteen years old and Blanche de Castille, both French and Southern civil and religious powers vowed to respect this treaty. There is a mystery here: why did Raymond VII accept to do so when the clauses which condemned the dynasty of Saint-Gilles were completely left out of the draft document agreed in Meaux in the previous January?

church by Guilhabert de Castres with the help of Raymond de Péreille and Pierre-Roger de Mirepoix in the face of these dangers. At the end of the summer of 1240, Trencavel returned. He had taken refuge in Aragon since 1229 and tried, with the help of other *faidits* including Olivier de Termes, Pierre de Fenouillet and Chabert de Barbaira to reconquer his land. At the head of a group that included a strong contingent of *Almogavares*, Catalan mercenaries whose reputation as fierce fighters was unsurpassed, he crossed the Corbières. He laid siege to Carcassonne from 7 September to 11 October after taking Limoux, Montolieu, Montréal and Saissac. However, learning of the arrival of royal forces, he escaped and took refuge in Montréal from which he only came out after bargaining to be exiled once again. The royal army, encouraged by this, and led by Jean de Beaumont, took some towns such as Laroque-de-Fa, defended by Olivier de Termes, and Peyrepertuse which capitulated after three days of siege on 16 November 1240.

Mirepoix: the cathedral

Montréal: the collegiate church

Avignonet: the crusader

Montségur: Tower Rock

Montségur: courtyard
and keep

42

16 March 1244...

Raymond VII did not aid Trencavel, but he did not collaborate with Louis IX either, who held this against him. The king called him to Montargis on 14 March 1241 reminding him of his commitments and asking him to destroy Montségur which Raymond VII then besieged without conviction or results. It was true that Raymond VII was also fermenting a coalition between the French crown and in particular Hugues de Lusignan, Count of La Marche, and Henry III of England. The latter landed in Royan on 20 May 1242. During the night of the 28 to 29 May, in Avignonet, the inquisitor Guillaume Arnaud and eleven Dominicans and Franciscans were assassinated with axes by a commando force of men who had come from Montségur and were led by Raymond d'Alfaro, the son-in-law of Raymond VI. A wind of revolt blew over the Midi. Raymond VII was excommunicated and the coalition in which he had actively participated fell apart after the battle of Taillebourg in July 1242. Definitively beaten, he surrendered to Louis IX and signed the peace of Lorris in January 1243. He appealed against his excommunication at the Council of Béziers which in fact decided on the fate of Montségur: "we must cut off the head of the dragon". Montségur held nearly five hundred people at the summit of the *pog* who were firm in their support of the siege which was coming. It lasted ten months and was led by the Seneschal of Carcassonne Hugues des Arcis who led an army of one thousand five hundred men. The *Mont sûr* resisted but, a short while before Christmas, after a small group of *basques* had climbed the Tower Rock and taken up the position, the besiegers were able to install their catapults. Immediately the situation became unbearable for the besieged and on 2 March 1244, Montségur surrendered. After a truce of fifteen days, the Cathars who refused to recant were condemned and on 16 March more than two hundred of them were to die on a pyre at the foot of the *pog*.

A time of pardon

In 1232, Gregory IX gave the mission of the Inquisition to the Dominican order and placed this extraordinary jurisdiction outside the ecclesiastical hierarchy. Its purpose was to eradicate heresy. This parallel religious power investigated, judged and condemned with canonical principles which, at the time, were added to by rules and practices listed in the inquisition manuals. Upon arrival in a town or village, an inquisitor proclaimed *tempus gratiae*, a period during which the believers of the heretics, or those who had dealt with them, were invited to repent, which avoided condemnation. The information collected completed that given by informants. God forbid a heretic who had not taken the opportunity of this time of pardon – he was guilty and could in no circumstances have the help of a lawyer. If at the end of an interrogation led by the inquisitor, who was armed with the procedures and a past master in handling theological subtleties, the heretic admitted his error, he had to do penance by fasting, prayer, pilgrimage or imprisonment in the *Mur*, the Inquisition prison or indeed wear the yellow cross. If the heretic disagreed with the accusation, he was condemned to the pyre and delivered into the hands of the secular arm which executed the sentence. These sentences were passed in a very theatrical way during the *general admonition* which the inquisitor gave before leaving the area. From 1252, with the agreement of Innocent IV, the trials of the Inquisition could make use of the Ordalie, a physical trial under the name of preliminary torture or interrogation. For one century, the Inquisition raged in Occitania, a trial of terror which would go as far as to order exhumations and burning of dead bodies.

The last of the Cathars

After the fall of Montségur, the Cathars, if they were not exiled to Lombardy or Catalonia, became clandestine. Raymond VII carried the mark of his defeat to the end of his life. He tried to remarry to have a son who could save his dynasty. He even participated in a pilgrimage to Compostella. In 1249 in a last cruel and useless gesture, he was responsible for the death of eighty Cathars on a pyre in Agen. He died in the same year in Millau while preparing finally to leave for the Holy Land. He was buried in Fontevault. His daughter Jeanne having married the brother of Louis IX, Alphonse de Poitiers in 1237, the latter became Count of Toulouse. In 1246 Trencavel had abandoned his rights to the crown of France for good. Fenouillèdes remained, where two fortresses resisted, but Puilaurens eventually surrendered and Quéribus laid down arms in 1255. As for Aragon, in the treaty of Corbeil in 1258 it renounced it sovereignty over all the land to the north of the Agly. When Jeanne and Alphonse de Poitiers died without any children in 1271, all of the Languedoc became part of the kingdom of France without need of sanction. As for the heresy, hunted, it had its last dramas and some surprises. In Italy, two hundred heretics captured in Sirmione in 1276 were burnt in the arenas of Verona on 13 February 1278. In the Languedoc, Pierre Authié, a Cathar *parfait*, preached and consoled on the roads in the Sabarthès area from 1299 to 1309. However the Inquisition pursued their sinister work, Innocent IV in 1252 having even authorized them to recourse to torture. One voice was raised, in 1302 against this abuse, that of the Franciscan Bernard Délicieux. Torture and prison broke him in 1320. The Cathar heresy was finally vanquished. Guillaume Bélibaste, the last known *parfait* was identified in Morella by a spy, Arnaud Sicre, and was captured and condemned to the pyre in 1321 in Villerouge-Termenès.

Bounty hunter

The members of his family were heretical believers: his maternal uncle, Pons Bayle, had been a *parfait* and a companion of Pierre Authié and his mother Sibille had died on the pyre. Perhaps it was with an idea of getting back the possessions confiscated from his mother, that Arnaud Sicre thought of a way to hunt out the Cathars who had taken refuge in Catalonia, to inform on them, for a reward, to the Inquisition. At the end of 1317, this son of a lawyer from Ax-les-Thermes went to San Mateo where he was welcomed by the heretics of the Sabarthès who were already living there and who introduced him to Guillaume Bélibaste. His family references could leave no doubt about his convictions. A year later, Arnaud Sicre came back to the area. His declared intention was to bring his aunt and sister to Catalonia. However he stopped in Pamiers at the house of Jacques Fournier, the then bishop of the town, to denounce Bélibaste. For the man who was in charge of the Inquisition, the news was important and to capture Bélibaste would be the final eradication of a heresy of which "Monsieur de Tortosa" was the last *parfait*. Jacques Fournier gave money to Sicre who had a plan to bring Bélibaste back to the north of the Pyrenees. It was in December 1320 that Sicre returned to Catalonia. He managed to convince Bélibaste to accompany him onto Languedoc soil to see his aunt, a believer, who was too old to come to Catalonia. It was near Castelbon, on the lands of the Count of Foix, that Bélibaste was captured with his companions in the early spring of 1321. On 21 October 1321, Jacques Fournier recorded the report of Arnaud Sicre who he congratulated and Bélibaste mounted the pyre of Villerouge-Termenès...

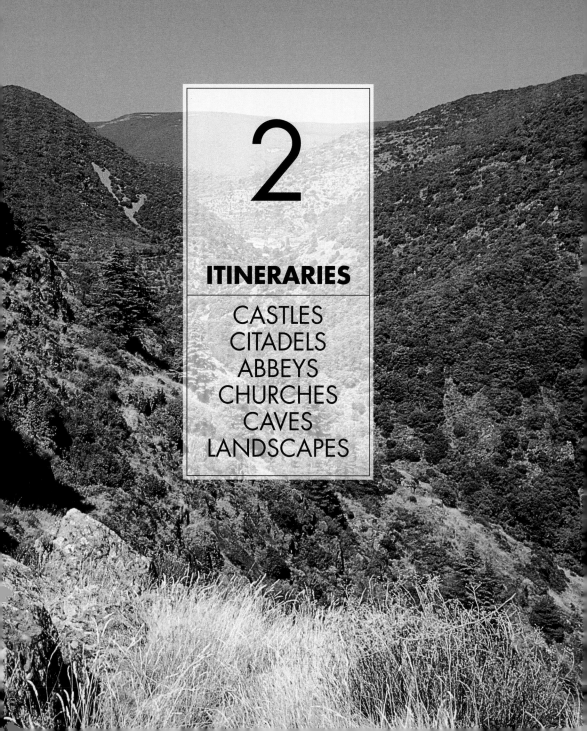

2

ITINERARIES

CASTLES
CITADELS
ABBEYS
CHURCHES
CAVES
LANDSCAPES

THE ALBIGEOIS, TOULOUSAIN AND LAURAGAIS AREAS

Albi

It was Innocent V who named Bernard de Castanet bishop of Albi in 1276 to a see which had been vacant for five years. Bernard de Castanet decided as soon as he arrived on the banks of the river Tarn to build a new cathedral, Saint Cecilia's, and have Berbie Palace finished, which had been started by his predecessor, Bernard de Combret. Work on the cathedral, started in 1282, lasted for more than a century. The new bishop was taking charge of his diocese more than a hundred years after the conference of Lombers had taken place there in 1165, near Albi, which was the origin of the Cathars being called Albigensians and nearly fifty years after Montségur. Nevertheless the heresy was still firmly rooted. It would find in the new bishop a man who would put all his zeal to work to subdue it. Castanet accepted that a Dominican convent should be built in Albi and in 1285 Jean Galand, an inquisitor who had come from Carcassonne, moved into the Palace of Berbie. In 1286 and 1287, the two men led the trial of eleven bourgeois who, during their interrogations gave the names of more than four hundred believers of the heresy. Bernard de Castanet organized a second trial in 1299 and 1300, after which thirty-five heretics, some tortured, were condemned to the *Mur Strict* or Strict Walls prison. The excesses of the Inquisition were criticized by Bernard Délicieux. When he was arrested in 1317, Castanet, who had become Cardinal of Oporto, and a famous inquisitor, the former prior of the preachers of Albi, Bernard Gui, led his trial. Catharism was eradicated in the Albi area and the massive silhouette of Saint Cecilia's Cathedral still bears witness to the victory of the orthodox church.

Bernard Délicieux

After the Albi trial in 1287, inquisitors came back to Carcassonne. In 1291, the inhabitants decried excesses to Philip the Fair who calmed their zeal. In 1295, Nicolas d'Abbeville recommended the activities of the trial and the people revolted. The inquisitors went to the Franciscan monastery where the leaders had taken refuge. Bernard Délicieux, the reader of the monastery, refused them entry. In 1297, d'Abbeville wanted to put on a posthumous trial of Castel Fabre, a bourgeois suspected of heresy. In fact Castel Fabre, buried within the walls of the Franciscan monastery had died not receiving *consolamentum*, but as a Christian, surrounded by Franciscans. Délicieux defended the memory of the deceased. In 1301 he criticized the inquisition for abuse during an audience with the King. Royal investigators became interested in Bernard de Castanet who also had to face a revolt. Délicieux led a movement in Albi, Cordes and Carcassonne. In 1304, Philip the Fair came here to resolve the question but disappointed Délicieux who tried, with the consuls of Carcassonne to put Languedoc in the hands of Ferrand, the Infante of Majorca. King James II of Spain, informed of the plan, told the king of France. The guilty were condemned, and some hung. Délicieux was delivered into the hands of Pope Clément V and lived as his dependant. In 1310, he went to Béziers. However his adversaries had not forgotten him. In 1317, Jean XXII had him arrested and tried in 1319, in Castelnaudary. Under torture he was condemned to the *Mur Strict* prison where he died in 1320.

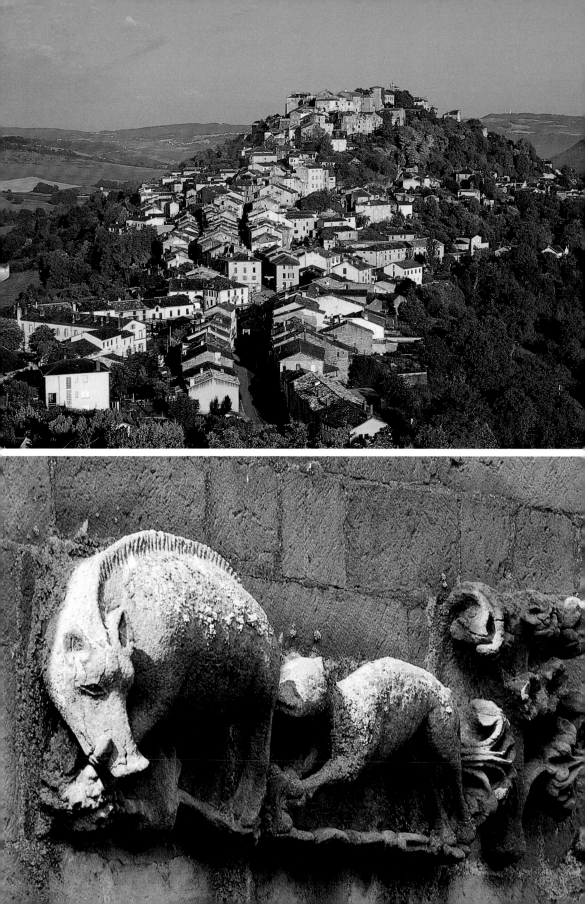

Cordes

It was in 1222 that the bastide of Cordes was founded by Raymond VII of Toulouse. The town grew quickly due to the number of Cathar weavers who, attracted by the privileges granted to them, moved there. This did not escape the eyes of the Inquisition. Legend tells that during revolutionary movements which interested the inquisitors, at the end of the 13th century, three Preaching Brothers were thrown by the inhabitants into a well which today is surmounted by a wrought iron cross with a marble plaque engraved with a text describing the episode. Cordes received by the word of Bernard Gui, the collective pardon of the Catholic church in 1321. Albi and Carcassonne had officially entered the ranks of the orthodox church the year before. Cordes, whose name may come, like that of Cordoba, from the leather craftsmen there, then went through a period of great prosperity ended in the 15th and 16th centuries by two epidemics of the plague and the Wars of Religion. However, the town, clustered around the summit of Mordagne Hill with the Cérou river flowing at its foot, was a wonderful sight and, thereafter called Cordes-sur-Ciel or Cordes in the Sky, has preserved its medieval character, the Gates of La Jane and Les Ormeaux, a barbican and a widow's walk, remains of the city walls, a market-place near the famous well, Saint Michael's Church from the 13th century and above all, along Rue Droite, the main street, houses with beautiful carved façades from the 13th and 14th centuries, such as the House of the Great Falconer, the House of the Grand Ecuyer or Master of the Horse or even that of the Grand Veneur or Master of the Hounds. On the façade of the latter, on the second floor, is a carved frieze in high relief representing hunting scenes: a hunter is preparing to throw his spear at a boar which is chasing a dog, another hunter is blowing his horn while another is aiming an arrow at a hare which has knocked down his dog…

Bastides

In order to promote the peace of God, the Church created in the 12th century places of safety, lands of asylum. A place of safety could be transformed into a *villeneuve*, an area for habitation which benefited from franchises and tax advantages. The *villeneuve* allowed its founder to occupy a deserted or uncertain region, to establish economic development there and to organize its reclamation. In the 13th century, in Aquitaine and the Languedoc, bastides developed, from 1222 onwards, the year in which one of them, Cordes was founded by Raymond VII of Toulouse. Bastides were a means, for their promoters, of reinforcing their power from an economic point of view, by acquiring rights and revenues from them, but also from a political point of view, by having better control of the population who were then regrouped and by placing these new towns within the limits of their possessions. An act of pareage and a charter of customs were at the forefront of the creation of a bastide. By the act of pareage the owner, whether civil or religious, of the land would give it over to county or royal agents who would organize the settlement. The charter offered newcomers safety and the possibility of success. At the death of Raymond VII, Alphonse de Poitiers, brother of Louis IX, took possession of the county of Toulouse and founded no less than thirty-six bastides. The Plantagenets created some in Aquitaine like Beaumont and Monpazier. Generally the bastide was built to an orthogonal design, around a central square, its streets making up a chessboard pattern. This urban type infrastructure distinguished it from a village and also from the *circulade*, from the 11th and early 12th century with its circular design, of which Bram was the archetypical example.

Toulouse

The little ford, the *badaculum*, the Bazacle, allowed the Garonne river to be crossed in times of low waters, and was at the origin of the creation of Toulouse by the Volques Tectosages in the 3rd century b.c. However in 118 b.c. they yielded to the Romans and *Tolosa* became a great Gallo-Roman town, even taking the title of Latin colony under the emperor Augustus. It was towards 260 a.d. that Saturnin, the first bishop of Toulouse, was put to death and in 418 the Visigoths made Toulouse the capital of their realm. After the defeat of the Visigoths in Vouillé in 507, Toulouse became Frankish and became calm for a while. From the 11th century, increases in the population gave Toulouse back the status of a large town, which had been somewhat lost. In the 12th century, the inhabitants of Toulouse, wine or salt merchants or leather craftsmen, cobblers and shoe-makers, made their town, a stopping place on the road to Compostella, a great financial centre where guaranteed loans built fortunes. In 1152, having economic power, these merchants and financiers entered the common council which balanced the political council of the Counts of Toulouse. These consuls eventually took the name of *senhors del Capitol*, lords of the chapter, and gave the Commune House or town hall its name of the Capitole.

It was in the same century that the scene for the Cathar drama was set. "*Que de totas ciutatz es cela flors e roza*". "For of all towns, it is the flower and the rose". So spoke Guillaume de Tudèle, the author of the *song of the crusade*, and he must be believed since he was not suspected of sympathies either with the Cathars or with the inhabitants of Toulouse. Were not these immigrants, who had come from the Lauragais area in the last few years and been establishing themselves in the suburb of Saint-Sernin where both spiritual and material riches were concentrated, bearers of heresy? Did they

Toulouse: the walkway of the Bazacle

not find a climate of tolerance in Toulouse? And the town's unity was sealed by the language of Oc, common to the southern lands and its faithfulness to the dynasty of Saint-Gilles. Toulouse was directly concerned by the Cathar heresy, the crusade against the Albigensians and its consequences, in the 12th and 13th centuries. In 1145, Bernard was received by the canons of Saint-Sernin and participated in a contradictory debate with the heretic Henri de Lausanne. In 1178, the abbot of Cîteaux, Henri de Marcy, also at Saint-Sernin, convinced Pierre Maurand, a Cathar, to be reconciled with the church. Another Cistercian, Foulque, became bishop of Toulouse in 1204 and remained so until 1229; it was he who decided on the enlarging of Saint Steven's Cathedral; it was also he who, at the head of the White Brotherhood, came to the support of the crusaders at the siege of Lavaur in 1211. A few months later, on 17 June, Simon de Montfort made Toulouse suffer its first siege. In the house of Pierre Sellan, Dominic founded the Dominican Order in 1215. After the death of its founder in 1233, the order was entrusted with the responsibility of the Inquisition and the building of Jacobins Church was undertaken. During the siege of Beaucaire in 1216, the inhabitants of Toulouse had revolted, Montfort had returned in great haste to the banks of the Garonne and severely repressed the movement after having denounced, in Saint Pierre des Cuisines, the amnesty promised by Foulque. On 13 September 1217, Raymond VI re-entered his town over the Bazacle and chased the crusaders, some of whom took refuge in Saint Steven's Cathedral, down Rue Croix-Baragnon. Montfort's family and supporters were protected by the walls of Narbonne Castle. Simon de Montfort then began the second siege of Toulouse and died at its walls on 25 June 1218. In 1219, Prince Louis undertook the third siege of Toulouse, but without success. Ten years later, the council of Toulouse ratified, in his own town, the surrender of Raymond VII.

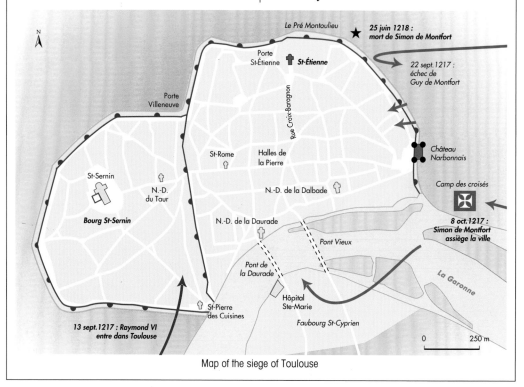

Map of the siege of Toulouse

From Courtly Love to Floral Games...

L anguedoc and Toulouse society before the crusade against the Albigensians took delight in the literary style of the *trobar*, the poetic inspiration from which the beautifully rhythmic verses written in the Oc language were found (from the verb *trouver*, to find). In this way the Oc language was lifted to the level of a true literary language. The troubadours, Peire Vidal and then Raimon de Miraval "only troubled with Love" and appealed to the same public as the Cathar *parfaits*. If there was no direct link between troubadours and Cathars, a parallel can be made between the search for evangelical purity on the one hand and the Ideal of Love and courtesy on the other. Raimon de Miraval, born in 1135, had a small castle, Caberdès. He was the protégé and friend of the Count of Toulouse and Peter II of Aragon, and sang Fine Amour, the poetic sentiment that could only lead to the spread of Good. "From Love come all my thoughts/I only trouble with Love/And all that is done for Love is good." This Love full of gentleness, slight eroticism, tender desire and joy was dedicated to the famous Lady Louve, Na Loba de Pennautier, the wife of one of the lords of Cabaret. However the fragile balance of Occitan society between the requirements of religious purity and the impetus of Fine Amour threatened to be broken forever by the French crusade in the Languedoc. Miraval then called on his friend, the King of Aragon and in 1213 still hoped that the crusaders would be chased out of the South: "Then Ladies and lovers can find once again

the joy of Loving that they have lost". The seizure by the French monarchy of the south had been a fact for a long time. Occitan language and culture then seemed so threatened that seven Toulouse troubadours formed the *Consistori de la subregaya companhia del Gay Saber* in 1323, which organized a poetry competition with the aim of "maintaining" the literary traditions in the Oc country. The first competition took place on 3 May 1324 and the winner, Arnaud Vidal of Castelnaudary, received a golden violet as his prize. The works presented dealt with religious themes or historical subjects among which the Western crusades had pride of place, speaking in praise of the kings or town-councillors or even describing the daily life of inhabitants of Toulouse. The competition became known as the *Jocs Florals* or Floral Games of Toulouse, and had considerable success, increased by the invention in the 15th century of the beautiful lady of legend, Clemence Isaure, who was said to have been the inspired sponsor and muse of the games. When Ronsard received the golden eglantine of the Floral Games of 1554, French had already taken over and when Louis XIV created the Académie des Jeux Floraux in 1694 with a wave of his sceptre, the language of the troubadours was relegated to the sad place of a regional dialect. However the literary tradition of the *Jocs Florals* had already been copied over the Pyrenees by Violante de Bar, queen of Catalonia and Aragon and wife of Joan I who had a poetry competition organized in Barcelona in 1393. The first prize had become a *flor natural*, a real flower. Here no golden violets, it was not necessary to keep the proof of a glory which, in any case, would be eternal.

The Florals Games, by Jean-Paul Laurens, Capitol, Toulouse

The Lauragais Area

At the crossing of the roads which led from the Languedoc to Aquitaine and from the Pyrenees to the Black Mountain, Catharism had spread throughout the Lauragais area and many inhabitants of villages such as Le Mas-Saintes-Puelles, Laurac, and Saint-Paul-Cap-de-Joux were believers in the heretical ideas. This area, with a peaceful landscape of rolling hills, therefore found itself at the very heart of the tragic events of the crusade against the Albigensians.

It was in Saint-Félix-Lauragais that the Cathar council of 1167 was held; the Cathar bishops of Albi, Agen and Carcassonne were ordained there by the Bogomil deacon Nicetas from whom they also received the *consolamentum*. Lavaur, whose Gothic Saint Alan's Cathedral, built in the 13th century, marked the triumph of the Catholic faith over the Cathar heresy, had received the visit in 1181 of the cardinal of Albano. The town was besieged in May 1211 by Simon de Montfort. Sixty Cathars met their end a few days later on the pyre at Les Cassés where a cross commemorates their martyrdom. It was near Montgey that the German crusaders who were awaited as reinforcements by Simon de Montfort's troops were massacred by Roger-Bernard, the Count of Foix and Guirard de Pépieux. In Castelnaudary one of the most famous battles of the crusade took place in 1211. After the failure of the third siege of Toulouse by Prince Louis in 1219, the future Raymond VII left on a campaign in the Lauragais. He took Lavaur in the spring of 1220 and then Puylaurens before entering Castelnaudary without any resistance, where he was besieged for eight months by Amaury de Montfort. It was on 20 July, during an attack that Guy, brother of Amaury, died of his wounds. On 28 May 1242 in Avignonet the inquisitors Guillaume, Arnaud, Etienne and their entourage were killed with axes.

The country of cocagne

With Toulouse, Albi and Carcassonne forming the corners, the *triangle du bleu*, or blue triangle, centred on the Lauragais, produced thirty to forty thousand tonnes of *agranat* every year during the 16th century. Agranat was a blue dye powder, extract of woad of which the long and thick leaves contain a good proportion of indigo starch. It was ground under the toothed millstone of the woad mill, moulded into balls – the famous *cocagnes* –, dried in the *agrenoir*, then reduced to powder, finally ready for use and sale after highly meticulous work taking six months. The opulent residences of the Toulouse woad merchants like Jean Bernuy or Pierre d'Assézat bear witness to the riches made from this trade, which made the expression *pays de cocagne* enter the lexical field synonymous with prosperity and opulence. The expression then meant "Land of Plenty" as well as referring to the balls of woad. Magrin Castle houses the Woad Museum, the only one of its kind in France. A woad mill has been rebuilt, near an authentic woad drier, the *agrenoir*, with its long net racks where the *cocagnes* of woad used to be dried.

Magrin, Woad Museum: the *cocagne* drier

The Canal joining the two seas

To cross by a waterway, the narrowest isthmus separating the Atlantic and the Mediterranean was, since ancient times, the dream of many men. The under-lessee for the Languedoc, Paul Riquet was to realise this dream… in less than fifteen years! Riquet described his project to Colbert, the Controller-General of finances for the Sun King, who made the southern tax-collector's obsession ridiculous. However, Louis XIV, who wanted to leave works worthy of his glory and greatness in his kingdom, gave his support to Riquet in 1666, while all Versailles laughed at "Riquet's ditch". Immediately, with the technical means of the time, one of most grandiose works of the century was undertaken. Everything was difficult: finding the money, the men, technical solutions. The canal had to be dug, levelled, adapted to the ground and water to feed it had to be found, particularly during the long summer months. Locks had to be included and designed and even a flight of locks when the slopes were too great. The canal also had to be filled with water. This was certainly the most difficult part of the project. Riquet knew the climate and hydrology of the region well. The Black Mountain nearby was a veritable water tower. He therefore decided to dig a *water store*, what we would today call a adjustment reservoir. His choice would be the Little Laudot at Saint-Ferréol. A wall thirty-five metres high would soon block the valley, and the reservoir, opened in 1672, covered an area of sixty-seven hectares and had a volume of 6 300 000 cubic metres of water. It was a great feat! At the time, no-one hesitated to make it the new and eighth wonder of the world! The Canal du Midi from Toulouse to the Mediterranean was to cross the famous Narouze Sill. This area of low hills, between the Pyrenees to the south and the Massif Central to the north, had always been the obligatory passage between the Mediterranean and the Atlantic. Riquet was not mistaken: his direction crossed this pass; an obelisk was built in 1827 to commemorate this colossal work. What

Cesse canal-bridge

Guerre Lock near Saint-Martin-Lalande

is, without doubt, the most beautiful and noblest work of this type ever undertaken". He suggested some improvements and they were carried out by Antoine Niquet, including: Cammazes Tunnel, the Cesse and Orbiel canal-bridges. The canal was not only useful for transporting goods. As soon as it was opened, a service of *post boats* was organized for passengers between Toulouse and Agde. The trip took four days and the stops were well planned. Dinner and a place to sleep was organized in inns often located near locks, with stables and chapels. A work of construction, the Canal du Midi is also a work of art. Lined with three-hundred year old trees, intersected by its locks (there are sixty-three of them), held up by its strong canal-bridges and crossed by stone bridges, the Canal du Midi is a magnificent architectural work which, since 1996 has been included in the world heritage of man by Unesco. What matter, after all, that our enormous barges or *péniches* can no longer travel along it! *Pénichettes* have replaced them, carrying tourists along the canal, the witness of an era when water coaches went at the speed of a walking horse.

ains he took! What a worry! Riquet, icknamed the "Moses of the Languedoc", acrificed everything for his work: his me, his fortune and his life. He died in 680, before the canal, his canal, was ompletely finished. By the following year, had been filled with water and the first arges, leaving from Toulouse, were able o go, without hindrance as far as Sète, wo hundred and forty kilometres further. auban inspected the canal in 1686 and eclared "The canal joining the two seas

Cammazes Tunnel

Pierre Paul Riquet

Saint-Papoul

Founded in the Carolingian Age and first dedicated to Saint Peter, the abbey of Saint-Papoul was subsequently dedicated to Saint Sernin of Toulouse, who evangelized the Lauragais. This abbey opted for the Rule of Saint Benedict at the beginning of the 11th century and became part of the property of the Abbey of Alet in 1119. It was in the early 12th century that the abbey church was built and at the beginning of the 14th century it became the see of a bishopric.

The abbey church has a single nave. It is rather wide and above has a barrel vault resting on ceiling beams. The apse, in cul-de-four, is surrounded by two side apses of which one has been lengthened in order to form a chapel adjoining the capitular chamber. The capitals in the side apses are simple in style; one of them represents a man with a wooden leg, the symbol of the unbeliever mutilated by sin. Outside, the apse is against five columns topped with capitals: two, historiated, show Daniel in the den where seven lions only lick him while the saint is pulling the prophet Habakuk's beard as he is bringing food, and some lions are devouring men, other capitals are just carved with acantha; the cornice is decorated with modillions some of which are carved with faces, including a man with a beard and moustache. These sculptures were carried out in the late 12th century by the Master of Cabestany, in contrast to the very worn ones in the side apses, which are in fact from the same era.

In the 14th century, the building of the cloister was begun. It opens onto the garden through semi-circular arches which are supported on twin columns topped with carved double capitals: some are historiated and others decorated with leaves or animals.

Saint-Papoul suffered the pillages of mercenaries in the 14th century, and then destruction caused in the 16th century by the Wars of Religion.

A capital from the choir: the man with the wooden leg

A capital from the apse by the Master of Cabestany

Fanjeaux

The Romans had erected a temple dedicated to Jupiter on this rising ground between Razès and the Lauragais. Its name was *Fanum Jovis* which gave its name to the village. At the end of the 12th century, Fanjeaux, like Montréal and Bram was largely won over by heretical ideas. Cathar communities had been established there and they worked in weaving and dyeing workshops. The co-lords of the *castrum* of Fanjeaux, Lady Na Cavaers and Guillaume de Durfort were also Cathars. The Durforts had a castle in the Termenès and Guillaume de Durfort was a troubadour. In 1204, Guilhabert de Castres who had lived in Fanjeaux since 1193, ordained as *parfaits* two of the ladies of Fanjeaux as well as Esclarmonde, the sister of the Count of Foix. It was to attack the heresy where it was most deeply rooted that in 1206 Dominic Guzmán chose Fanjeaux as the central point for his campaign of preaching. Tradition has it that he lived in the house so-called Saint Dominic's House. In 1209, Simon de Montfort and his crusaders invaded Montréal and Fanjeaux where the military chief of the crusade met Dominic who even became parish priest of Fanjeaux in 1214. When the military head of the crusade arrived the inhabitants fled. The village had other tragic moments since in 1355 it was burnt by the Black Prince's armies.

There are no remains of the medieval castle and fortifications; the so-called Sicaire cross opposite the church is said to have been found in the place where the Miracle of Saint Dominic took place. When leaving Fanjeaux, on the road leading to Montréal there is a 13th century cross on the parapet of a bridge. It has been attributed to the Cathars but it seems certain that the physical representations of the so-called "Bogomil" themes, and also the Greek crosses within a circle or the circular Occitan crosses have been wrongly attributed to the Cathars.

Dominic, Preaching Friar

It was after having seen a fireball fall three times on Prouille from the Seignadou Promontory which overlooks Bram Plain to the east of Fanjeaux that Dominic founded Prouille Monastery in 1207. Nine Cathar women that he had converted were received there. Dominic participated in several "disputes", meetings where heretics and Catholics discussed their opposing theological arguments. The dispute of Montréal in the spring of 1207, was one of the most famous. Four referees had to examine the reports of each side. The idea came to the Catholics to give these antinomic texts the ordeal by fire. Dominic's page, thrown into the flames three times, did not burn and got stuck on a ceiling beam which partly burned. Legend has it that the half-burnt beam built into the wall of a chapel in Fanjeaux church is one and the same. On the other hand, the page of the Cathar *parfaits* was completely destroyed. When in 1209 arms became the only arguments, Dominic was a constant support for the crusaders' camp. Faced with the increasing strength of the heresy, he founded the "Dominican Order" in 1215 whose rule was approved in 1216 by Pope Honorius III. Dominic died in 1221. His order was given the command of the Inquisition Tribunal by Pope Gregory IX in 1233.

Saint Dominic

2

THE ARIEGE AREA

Mirepoix

During the 13th century, Mirepoix housed Cathar heretics who created several houses of *parfaits* there. The lord of the town, Pierre-Roger de Mirepoix, himself, was a Cathar. It was in Mirepoix in 1206 that six hundred Cathars participated at a council and asked Raymond de Péreille to rebuild the defences of Montségur Castle. When the town was besieged in 1209, most of the heretics had already taken flight to the nearby mountain. After the town had been invaded, Guy de Lévis, a crusader knight and faithful lieutenant of Montfort, moved to Mirepoix in order to control the pass between the Pyrenean chain and the Garonne plain. The town was taken in March 1223 by Raymond-Roger de Foix but came back to the Lévis family after the Meaux Treaty. In 1289 a flood destroyed Mirepoix which was then on the right bank of the Hers. Legend associated this event to the disappearance of Puivert Lake which was said to have suddenly been emptied. Jean de Lévis had a bastide rebuilt in a safer place at the confluence of the Hers and the Countirou.

This small town clinging to the foot of the Pyrenean chain still has an almost completely medieval character. The main square is surrounded by wooden arches topped with magnificent half-timbered houses. The beams of the House of the Consuls are still almost intact and have incredible sculptures of human heads and hideous monsters at their ends. Saint Maurice's Cathedral was consecrated in 1298 and important restoration was carried out in 14th and 15th centuries. Its very wide Gothic nave posed many problems when the roof was finished… in the 19th century!

Cathar Society

Interrogations led by the Inquisition in the Languedoc gave a fairly precise idea of the spread of Catharism in Occitan society. It seems that the heresy had spread to leading citizens of the town; merchants, financiers, comfortably-off craftsmen, men of law and even royal officers, and the less important town and country knights or even the noble classes to which Pierre Roger de Mirepoix, a convinced Cathar, belonged. The Cathar *parfaits* had to work. A great cloth-making region in the Middle Ages, the number of Languedoc weaving workshops increased and became, during the 13th century, centres of proselytism. In Mas-Cabardès, the Weavers' Cross was considered by some to be of Cathar origin. This is very uncertain, but the fact that it was suggested indicates that there was definitely a link between the profession and the heresy, to such a point that *tesseyre*, weaver in Occitan, quickly became a synonym of Cathar. If many weavers were Cathars perhaps the solution can be found in the fact that Saint Paul had this profession and the tranquil, meditative life that they led, as René Nelli pointed out. Basket-weaving, leatherwork and medicine were also activities practised by *parfaits*. As for female *parfaits*, they were educated or indeed cultured and directed *maisons* or houses, a sort of convent where young Cathar girls were brought up and single women took shelter. Work was their main activity, whatever their social background.

Along the River Hers, from the source to the Ariege Valley

The Hers, a tributary of the Ariege, has its source in Drazet Fountain, not far from the Signal of Chioula. After passing near Montaillou Castle, the river enters the Frau Gorges, the Gorges of Fear. A few kilometres upstream from Bélesta, Fontestorbes Fountain is distinguishable, in dry weather by its intermittent flow: the water diminishes forhalf an hour and then rises for a quarter of an hour. The Hers makes a detour in the *département* of Aude and in Chalabre, receives the waters of the Blau which starts at the foot of the Sault Plateau. Every summer, a range of activities based on medieval themes demonstrations of

Chalabre Castle

Frau Gorges

knight hood, archery and weaponry takes place at the castle of Chalabre... The river flows an through Puivert. Legend has it that in Camon, the future Charlemagne himself founded an abbey in 778 that Philippe de Lévis bishop of Mirepoix lifted from its ruins. The latter belonged to the Lévis-Mirepoix family which received Lagarde Castle, former fief of the counts of Foix after the crusades, perched above the village which bears the same name. Guy de Lévis was a faithful crusader lord and close to Simon de Montfort. After taking Mirepoix, the chief of the crusade wanted to move to the region, a family clan which he could count on. The Lévis therefore

Lagarde Castle

became the Lévis-Mirepoixs. The defences of Lagarde Castle were reinforced by Guy III de Lévis-Mirepoix. After passing Mirepoix to the north, the Hers passes Vals, a former Celtic oppidum inhabited since ancient times. The Rupestrian church, partly buried in the soft rock, has been well arranged on two levels. The lower crypt is richly decorated with 12th century wall frescoes of Byzantine inspiration representing the life of Christ. The upper level dates from the Romanesque era and the bell-tower turret is decorated with a stone discoid grave-marker. Between Vals and the Hers-Ariege confluence, the bastide of Mazères was founded in 1252 on the land of Boulbonne Abbey. Like all bastides, it has a chessboard design with rectilinear streets at right angles. In the town centre is the church and the covered market with a beautiful roof structure. It is said that the famous Gaston III of Foix, better known as Gaston Fébus, received King Charles VI in his castle here. In honour of the sovereign's visit, he had all the cows' horns of an enormous herd painted blue as a reminder of the blazoning of his own coat of arms: "On gold with two red cows passant side by side, horned, hoofed and coloured with the blue that is from Béarn." The famous Gaston de Foix, Duke of Nemours was born in Mazères in 1489

Vals Church

and died in 1512 in Ravenna. Nearby, the castle and Cistercian abbey of Boulbonne were completely destroyed during the Wars of Religion. In the mid 12th century, the Count of Foix, Roger Bernard, was the benefactor of the abbey and granted it rights, privileges, land and rents. He made this abbey the *necropolis of the Counts of Foix*. Simon de Montfort came to shelter in Boulbonne on 10 September 1213 two days before the battle of Muret. At the end of the 13th century, the abbey included two future abbots of Fontfroide among its monks: Arnaud Nouvel and his nephew Jacques Fournier. Upstream of the Hers-Ariege confluence, on the banks of the latter, Pamiers owes its origins to its castle and the founding in the 10th century of an abbey dedicated to Saint Antonin of which almost nothing remains today. It was in 1111 that Roger II, count of Foix, decided to found Apamea Castle in memory of the Syrian town of the same name when he returned from the crusades. Only the *castella* remains, a green hillock on which the castle was erected. In the early 13th century, Esclarmonde de Foix, a Cathar *parfait*, stayed in Pamiers and Simon de Montfort had the famous articles written here in 1212.

Fresco 12 th century, Vals church

Foix

Esclarmonde, the sister of the Count of Foix was a Cathar *parfait*. Her brother, Raymond-Roger, if he was not a heretic, was, as early as 1209, one of the fervent partisans of the Occitan cause. He fought in Castelnaudary in 1211 and in Muret in 1213. His eloquence at the Council of Latran in 1215 allowed him to put his castle under the shelter of the Church. Nevertheless, Montfort, when he invaded the Foix area in 1217 to besiege Montgaillard, occupied Foix Castle. In September of that year, the Count of Foix participated in the Saint-Lizier conference; he died in 1223. His son, Roger-Bernard II entered Toulouse with Raymond VI in 1217 and was a faithful supporter of Raymond VII during the reconquest. After the Treaty of Meaux, the latter asked Roger-Bernard II to surrender, which he did in Saint-Jean-de-Verges on 16 June 1229. When Roger-Bernard III inherited the viscounty of Béarn in 1290, the lords of Foix-Béarn became very independent *Pyrenean Princes*. Their line included Gaston III of Foix-Béarn (1331-1391) known under the name of Gaston Fébus. Although abandoned to the profit of the Béarn fortresses, Foix preserved a military role due to its strategic position on the Franco-Aragon border. Finally the union of the Foix-Béarns with the Navarre family further reinforced the power of these southern lords. When Henri de Navarre became King of France under the name of Henri IV, the county of Foix was attached to the crown of France.

At the summit of its rocky outcrop, Foix Castle dominates the town. The primitive castle, with the two square towers and crenelated ramparts, appeared at the beginning of the 13th century under the seal of Roger Bernard, Count of Foix. The round tower completed the fortifications in the 15th century. Between Foix and Lavelanet, Roquefixade Castle was the subject of a dispute between Roger IV, Count of Foix and Raymond VII, Count of Toulouse, who became its direct suzerain in 1243.

Esclarmonde de Foix

Esclarmonde de Foix was the daughter of Roger-Bernard I de Foix and Cécile de Béziers. She was born around 1160. She married Jourdain II de l'Isle by whom she had six children. At his death, in 1200, she retired to Pamiers where her Cathar convictions were affirmed. She received the *consolamentum* in Fanjeaux in 1204 in the house of Guilhabert de Castres. She sold all her worldly goods and dedicated herself to her mission as a *parfait* in her *maison* in Pamiers where she received many Cathars. It is probable that among her possessions had been Montségur Castle which was then given to Raymond de Péreille and Pierre-Roger de Mirepoix for their keeping. It was in Pamiers Castle in 1207 that the conference opposing Cathars and Catholics, including the bishop of Osma, Dominic and Foulque was held, during which Brother Steven of Misericord cried "Really Madam, spin on your distaff, it ill becomes you to participate in such discussions". This is at least what is told in the *Chronicle* of Guillaume de Puylaurens who was close to Foulque, himself present at the conference. Some weight can be given to this quotation which shows an important point of disagreement among Cathars and Catholics regarding the place of women in society. After this date, there is no other mention of Esclarmonde, except by her brother, the Count of Foix during the Council of Latran who spoke of her in the imperfect tense. When and where did she leave this world? Perhaps after having had to escape from Pamiers which had fallen into the hands of Simon de Montfort in 1209. The first name of this great figure of Catharism was given by Raymond de Péreille to his own daughter who died in 1244 on the pyre at Montségur.

Painted caves in Ariege

More than 10 000 years ago, prehistoric man occupied the caves that nature had patiently shaped in the limestone layers of the Ariege mountains. The Magdalenian population, a culture from the Upper Palaeolithic Age from 18 000 to 12 000 b.c., occupied Bédeilhac Cave, Niaux Cave, La Vache and Le Tuc d'Audoubert Caves. Bédeilhac Cave, in the Arize mountain, opens with a porch of fifteen metres high and seven hundred and twenty metres long. Its amazing dimensions made it an aeronautical store during the second world war. Some even imagined that it had been used as a landing strip! 13 000 years ago, the Magdalenians decorated its walls with engravings, paintings and even low-reliefs in clay, such as a bison with a squat body. In the *Black Chamber* of Niaux Cave in Vicdessos Valley, other Magdalenians drew one of the masterpieces of prehistoric art in charcoal. Bison, horses, ibex and deer all come together... One bison has a body full of arrows; another is near an ibex. Niaux Cave are, with Lascaux and Altamira, among the great decorated caves of Southern Europe. The fragility of this underground place explains the creation of copies which allow an ever-increasing number of visitors to discover the masterpieces which have been preserved for thousands of years without the risk of losing the originals. The Pyrenean Park of Prehistoric Art near Tarascon-sur-Ariege is part of this action. At the heart of a maze plunged into darkness which reminds us of the underground world, the Great Workshop offers a path through the origins of art. Guided by information received through an infra-red headset, the visitor can admire on giant screens models, remains and copied drawings, expressing all the virtuosity of the Magdalenian artists from Niaux and

Pyrenean Park of Prehistoric Art: Traces waterfall

Niaux Cave, the Black Chamber: bisons

elsewhere. Outside, a leisure park shows a prehistoric scene strictly based on scientific foundations, and layout, size and sound create an *imaginary world*. Nearly opposite Niaux Cave are La Vache Cave. It is possible that the same men lived in these neighbouring places, using one shelter for daily life and the other for spiritual or even religious practices. Remains have been found in these caves, notably engraved bones, one showing a deer and fish. Near Saint-Girons, clay bison modelled by the Magdalenians have been found in Le Tuc d'Audoubert Caves. In the Plantaurel Massif, Le Mas-d'Azil Caves are crossed by the Arize. At the end of the Upper Palaeolithic Age, twelve thousand years b.c., this long and spacious tunnel was the cradle of a new culture which followed the Magdalenians. It was studied in the 19th century by Piette with the help of excavations carried out on the site and bears the

Le Tuc d'Audoubert: clay bison

name of Azilian culture. Climate conditions had changed; general warming led to the appearance of a damp temperate forest. Stone tools with scrapers, gravers and blades had evolved little. Nevertheless these men were innovative with their Azilian pointed tools with curved backs, sharpened at both ends. Bone tools were rarer but flat harpoons, with large teeth and perforations in the base were common. While their Magdalenian predecessors can be called artists, the Azilians lost this mastery of the sketch. They no longer drew on the walls of their caves. They barely decorated stones that they painted or engraved with geometric motifs, lines, dots, spots and scratches… The elements of their clothing were also less rich and apart from pierced or grooved teeth, few objects can be seen today.

Le Mas d'Azil: a spearthrower

The Sabarthès Area

The Cathar heresy was widely spread in the Sabarthès and the lords Raymond of Salles, of Lordat, or Arnaud of Miglos gave their support to the Cathar church, the second bringing war machines to the besieged of Montségur in 1243. All had to answer to the trials of the Inquisition. It was in Sabarthès that Catharism lasted for the longest time. Pierre Authié, a notary from Ax-les-Thermes, and his brother Guilhem left in 1296 for Lombardy where they met up with members of the Languedoc Cathar church who were exiled and welcomed by Italian Cathars, of whom two hundred who were captured in Sirmione in 1276 had died on the pyre built in the arena of Verona in 1278. They received the *consolamentum* there. When they returned to France at the end of 1299, the Authiés preached and gave the *consolamentum* in the Toulouse, Sabarthès and Razès areas. However, they were followed or even hunted down by the inquisitor Bernard Gui and were found and judged; they died on the pyre in 1310. For Pierre Authié the pyre was built on 9 April 1310 in front of Saint Steven's Cathedral in Toulouse. Jacques Fournier, abbot of Fontfroide, was named bishop of Pamiers in 1317 and in his diocese became the head of the Inquisition. From 1318 to 1325 he systematically interrogated the inhabitants of mountain villages with exceptional analytical finesse, such as those of Montaillou, in the county of Foix and Sabarthès. He then compiled a register, an exemplary document for historical research; Jean Duvernoy and Emmanuel Le Roy Ladurie, for his famous *Montaillou*, took the rich content of their work from this register. In 1334, Jacques Fournier became Pope in Avignon under the name of Benedict XII and did much building. The Old Palace, an austere fortress is owed to him, showing his taste for Cistercian sobriety coming from his former religious order.

The underground world

The patient work of the water dug out many caves in the subsoil of the Sabarthès area, the Arize massif and the Plantaurel mountain. Some were occupied by prehistoric man and others offer the beauty of their mineral decoration to those who visit them. The underground river of Labouiche, in the Plantaurel, has been cleared for a boat trip of one thousand five hundred metres. To the south of Tarascon-sur-Ariège, Lombrives Cave has an underground lake and natural concretions with evocative names: the Mammoth, the Petrified Waterfall... Legend had it that the tomb of Pyrene, who was in love with Hercules could be found there. A sheer rocky wall of fifty metres high blocks the gallery and makes access to the upper chambers difficult of which the opening can just be made out at the summit. Ladders must be used here. It was behind this wall that a heap of human skeletons was found. Was it by order of Caesar that Gaul tribes who had not surrendered were walled up like this? Some objects found among the bones lead us to suppose so. In any case, the cave was certainly the setting for dramatic events and the mystery of the collective death hangs over it.

Labouiche underground river

Montségur

The *pog* of Montségur, a limestone peak crowned with the ruins of the castle, ends at an altitude of 1208 metres in the heart of the Ariege Pyrenees in the Tabe Massif.

Around 1204, the rising peril became clear for the Cathar church. Innocent III became more and more pressing: he had just named Arnaud-Amaury, abbot of Cîteaux at the head of his legation in the Languedoc while soliciting the King of France Philip Augustus to intervene with the military. Six hundred Cathar *parfaits* therefore met at a council in Mirepoix after which, with a view to establishing a base to entrench themselves, the Cathar hierarchy asked Raymond de Péreille, co-lord of Lavelanet, to rebuild Montségur Castle which its lord admitted was "in a state of ruin". In the years that followed, Montségur was more or less used according to the political climate but in 1232, Guilhabert de Castres asked Raymond de Péreille if he could establish "the head and seat" of the Cathar church there. Two hundred men and women *parfaits* came to live there. In order to ensure its defence, Pierre-Roger de Mirepoix established a garrison of knights and squires and around fifty men-at-arms, all with their families. These men and women were Cathars and made up a united society, bound by the same convictions and family links or links of friendship. The five hundred people who made up this community lived in Montségur, divided among the castle itself and the small village which was built at the bottom of the ramparts on vertiginous terraces. Archaeological remains discovered on the site show intense human activity. A semblance of a siege without success was organized by Raymond VII in 1241 after the request made by Louis IX in Montargis. However the murder of the inquisitors at Avignonet, during the night of 20 May 1242, was the spark which lit the fire. The "head of the dragon" had to be "cut off",

Montségur Museum

Since 1958, the speleological society of the Ariege and GRAME (Archaeological Research Group for Montségur and surroundings) in co-operation with the National Centre for Cathar Studies have begun a serious research work on the site of Montségur. Montségur Archaeological Museum, inaugurated in 1986, exhibits pieces discovered during excavations. Two skeletons of those besieged take the visitor back in a poignant way to the heart of the drama of Montségur. Cannonballs remind us that at the time of the siege mangonels were used by both camps. However it is the domestic objects, oil lamps, pincers, keys and tailors' scissors which best show the life, at the summit of the *pog* of the men and women who took refuge there.

A golden metal crowned head, 13th century

decided the Council of Béziers in 1243. Seneschal Hugues des Arcis was asked to lead the siege; Pierre Amiel, the archbishop of Narbonne, was the spiritual leader of operations. The *Mont sûr* resisted, but shortly before Christmas 1243, a troop of *basques* climbed the Tower Rock during the night where those holding siege were able to install their snares. A believer, Mathieu, and a *parfait*, Pierre Bonnet, were able to escape Montségur with the treasure of the Cathar church, which they hid in a cave in the Sabarthès, perhaps the fortified *spoulga* of Bouan. Before the end of 1243, a ballistics expert arrived and had ballista built which allowed the besieged to respond. However the situation of the latter became more and more unbearable and on 2 March 1244, Montségur surrendered after a siege of ten months. After a respite of fifteen days, the Cathars who had refused to recant their faith were condemned and on 16 March more than two hundred of them died on a pyre which had been built at the foot of the *pog*. On the eve of the pyre, four Cathars managed to escape and go to Usson Castle where they were able to take back the treasure of the Cathar church which had been evacuated during the siege. After the drama, Montségur was given to Guy de Lévis by Louis IX and became a royal fortress. The castle was occupied until the 16th century and subsequently abandoned.

Lodged between rock and sky, the far-off walls crown the *pog* at the foot of which, in *Prat dels Cramats*, the Field of the Burnt Ones, a funeral grave-marker was built in memory of the Cathar martyrdom. A castle fortified even by nature due to its position, it seemed inaccessible and impregnable with the sheer sides of the *pog*, to which dense and highly perfumed box trees cling.

Contrary to the claims of some authors, Montségur Castle is not at all linked to a sun-worshipping sect. The Cathars knew nothing of such beliefs: rejecting the material world as work of Evil, they could not adore a solar star which shed light upon the sadnesses of that world! Indeed campaigns of excavations and work of medieval historians show that the present castle is later than the Cathar episode. In fact, if a certain geometry was used to build the castle, it was the result of methods of working, without any esoteric intention, the architects using ground plan and vertical measurements based on pre-established modules.

The design of the present castle is very simple. A single postern, a massive keep and its tank, walls reinforced by rock which surround a long central courtyard. When entering, the visitor feels protected by the high walls but also, perhaps, like the Cathar *parfaits* in the 13th century, a little isolated from the rest of the world, confined to a space of purity and perfection, entrenched in that which became the symbol of willing or even hoped for sacrifice, in opposition to the incomprehension of the powerful and the strong.

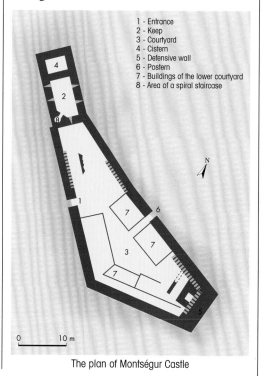

1 - Entrance
2 - Keep
3 - Courtyard
4 - Cistern
5 - Defensive wall
6 - Postern
7 - Buildings of the lower courtyard
8 - Area of a spiral staircase

The plan of Montségur Castle

3

QUERCORB, CORBIÈRES AND RAZÈS

Puivert

Puivert castle dates from the 14th century when the Bruyère family were its lords. In the 12th century, a primitive castle stood on this hill in the Quercorb area. In 1170, a meeting of troubadours was held here and during the summer of 1185, Trencavel and Loba, Lady of Cabaret, met for festivities. Courtly tradition was continued as can be seen in the Musicians Chamber in the eight pendants representing artists playing the instruments of the time. In November 1210 the castle was besieged by Montfort. It then belonged to the Congost family who were heretics. Alpaïs, mother of Gaillard, lord of Puivert, had received in 1208 the *consolamentum* of the dying. Congosts participated in the massacre of the inquisitors in Avignonet in 1242 and defended Montségur in 1244. Puivert fell after three days of siege. Legend tells that in 1279 an Aragon princess, the White Lady, had wished that the level of water in the lake at the foot of the castle could be lowered so that its banks would be more accessible. Did the work provoke this catastrophe? The flow swept away the princess and flooded Mirepoix and Chalabre.

On the east side, a tower-gate gives access to the lower courtyard which overlooks the keep by thirty-two metres. Above the door of the keep, the Bruyère family engraved their coat of arms, a lion rampant with a forked and knotted tail. The chapel, on the third level of the keep, below the musicians' chamber, has an ogival vault. The keystone of the arch is carved with a virgin and Michael fighting the dragon. The six mouldings rest on the pendants where strange personages are brandishing scrolls.

Quercorb Museum

In the village of Puivert, Quercorb Museum is an interesting addition to the castle visit with its history room where a model of the monument allows one to better understand it. In the *Instrumentarium* Room, there are moulds of eight sculptures of the musicians of the keep coming out of the night with rebuilt musical instruments: bagpipes, hurdy-gurdy, tambourine, lute, portable organ, psaltery, rebeck and cithern. The Quercorb in the 19th and early 20th century is shown through the life of its inhabitants. It was a cornerstone in the evolution of techniques and the economy, by changing the shape of artisans' activity, and generated a new society with makers of barrels or cattle-bells in Rivel, chair-makers, comb-makers in the Hers Valley, wood turners in Puivert and the blacksmiths and workers of jet.

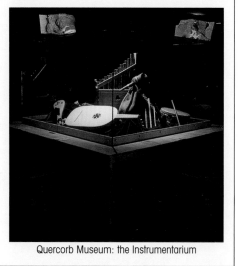

Quercorb Museum: the Instrumentarium

Usson

At the up-stream entrance to the Aude Gorges the castle of Usson is hidden amongst the narrow confines of this rocky landscape. From 1232 to 1244, protected by its isolation, this castle was practically an annexe of Montségur. The bishop of the Cathar Church in Toulouse, Guilhabert de Castres, and some other Good Men stayed there. During the siege the Lords Bernard d'Alion and Arnaud d'Usson, believing in the heretics, sent arms and reinforcements to the besieged. On 15 March 1244, the last day of the truce, before the pyre was lit, four *parfaits*, despite the vigilance of the besiegers, managed to escape in the rocky escarpments and leave the *pog*. At the price of much effort, the fugitives got back to Usson Castle where they were able to get back the Cathar treasure that had been evacuated from Montségur some days before Christmas 1243 by the *parfait* Pierre Bonnet accompanied by a believer, Mathieu.

The Aude Gorges

The Aude Gorges

The Aude is a Pyrenean torrent upstream of its course, and cuts a difficult path through the buttresses at the foot of the mountain. Saint George's Gorges, around three hundred and fifty metres deep and only twenty metres wide, have been dug out of thick layers of limestone by the river. The water then had to deal with another rocky barrier but has only been able to make a narrow passage. This is called the defile of Pierre-Lys and only a small ribbon of sky can be seen above the sheer vertical walls. Courage and time was needed by the parishioners of the priest Félix Armand de Saint-Martin-Lys at the end of the 18th century to build a road through here. Three tunnels were dug when the bed of the torrent was too narrow. Further downstream the Trou du Curé or Priest's Hole reminds us of these men who started an enormous work which was to be finished only in 1887 with just pickaxe and pick.

The Trou du Curé

Puilaurens

At the end of the 10th century, Puilaurens belonged to the abbey of Saint-Michel de Cuxa. The castle came under the influence of Aragon in 1162. Although it remained aloof of military operations such as the crusade against the Albigensians, it was a refuge for heretics and for *faidits*, lords such as Guillaume de Peyrepertuse, condemned by the Council of Toulouse in 1229 for his resistance in the *castrum* of Puilaurens. The lord of Fenouillet, who died in 1242 in the hands of the heretics was a Cathar and the fortresses that he still controlled, such as Puilaurens or Fenouillet, presented serious guarantees in the Fenouillèdes area argued over by the crowns of France and Aragon. His son Hugues de Saissac succeeded him but it was Chabert de Barbaira who took military command of the castles. How and when did this castle come back to the Capetians? Sources do not give precise answers to these questions but in 1255 while Quéribus was falling, Puilaurens had already entered the royal domain. In 1258, after the treaty of Corbeil, in which Aragon gave over to France all lands to the north of the Agly, Saint Louis and Philip the Bold had the fortifications of Puilaurens well reinforced and with Aguilar, Quéribus, Peyrepertuse and Termes, comprised an imposing line of defence of the south of the kingdom called "the five sons of Carcassonne". In 1260 the garrison of Puilaurens had only twenty-five sergeants. Occupied in 1635 by Spanish troops, Puilaurens lost all its strategic importance after the treaty of the Pyrenees in 1659 which moved the border with Spain from the Agly to the line of the crest of the Pyrenees. The castle was made into a prison for a while and then little by little abandoned to the violent assaults of the wind and the patient wear of time.

Puilaurens Castle crowns a rocky ridge 697 metres high which dominates the Boulzane Valley. This imposing site is surrounded by a cirque of mountains with slopes which are covered in conifers. The fortifications which can be seen today are mostly later than the treaty of Corbeil. In order to get to the door of the castle, after climbing through undergrowth, a series of walls arranged as a barrier must be crossed. Covered by a loophole flanking the south wall, the door, defended by a fall-trap, gives access to the lower courtyard, surrounded by curtain walls which are supported by the east and south towers and crossed by a widow's walk. A second wall, to the south-west, dominates the lower courtyard. It forms a triangle within which the keep rises at its centre and which has towers at its north-west and south-west corners. Near the entrance door to the south-west tower, called the White Lady's Tower, a voice tube drilled into the wall allows one to communicate with the upper floor where two benches frame the bay which opens to the south-east.

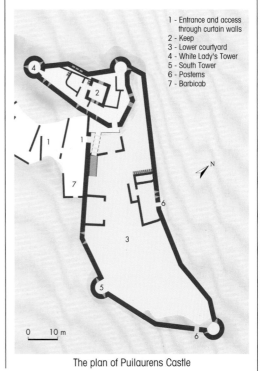

1 - Entrance and access through curtain walls
2 - Keep
3 - Lower courtyard
4 - White Lady's Tower
5 - South Tower
6 - Posterns
7 - Barbican

0   10 m

The plan of Puilaurens Castle

South of the Corbières and near Roussillon, Fenouillèdes

Fenouillèdes, a region of contrasts between the Corbières and Roussillon, presents an amazing landscape: verdant valleys where vines like those in Maury stretch out after rocky barriers, impregnable cliffs with giddy peaks. To the south of Caudiès-de-Fenouillèdes, the road goes up towards the south, goes around the hermitage of Notre-Dame de Laval, from where the characteristic silhouette of Bugarach Peak can be seen to the north, which at 1230 metres high is the culmination of the Corbières. Nearby stand the ruins of Fenouillet Castle. The aqueduct-bridge of Ansignan which crosses the Agly measures one hundred and seventy metres long. The water is taken one kilometre upstream and irrigates the lands of a *villa*, the property of a certain *Ansinius* from which the nearby village takes its name. Bélesta Caves, the *caune*, houses in one of its chambers a necropolis of around thirty people from the 4th century b.c. Bélesta Castle-Museum exhibits archaeological remains excavated from the caves at different times. The old hermitage of Força Réal, a belvedere, offers a view which

Ansignan Aqueduct-Bridge

stretches from the Canigou to the sea. It was in 1971 that Professor Henry de Lumley brought to light in the cave called Caune de l'Arago, the skull of Tautavel Man, so named after the village situated to the south of the Corbières near Estagel in a plain where vines grow. This *Homo erectus* occupied the site 450 000 years ago. A nomad hunter, *Homo erectus* lived in groups of about twenty individuals. His camp was chosen according to the presence of game, an important element in his food, that he hunted armed with a simple stick with a pointed end. His tools, carved from stone, allowed him to cut up

Tautavel Museum: the skull of Tautavel Man

Bélesta Castle-Museum: a sepulture

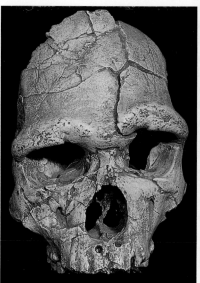

Galamus Gorges

his prey. However Tautavel Man had not yet learned the art of fire… The museum, where a whole room is dedicated to the techniques of excavation and methods of research is very educational as it uses modern and varied methods which make the visit most lively: reconstitutions of scenes from the life of Tautavel Man in slide shows, interactive multimedia points, audiovisuals including a wall of images. Caune de l'Arago and Tautavel Man are thus placed on a scale of time and Evolution. The Agly made a crack in the limestone chain of Lesquerde, the clue de la Fou, thus allowing communication from north to south, easy although tortuous, that was used by the Romans, as shown by the bridge that they built here. It is on these lands of a former Roman villa known by the name of *Monedarius* that Saint-Paul-de-Fenouillet can be found. At the end of the 10th century, there was already a monastery, Saint-Paul de Valolas here. In 1066 it adopted the Rule of Cluny. In 1318, the abbey became a collegiate church by a decision by Pope John XXII where a chapter of the diocese of Alet had its see. This chapter prospered and acquired goods, land and forests. The hermitage of Saint Antony, in the Galamus Gorges, was one of their possessions; they gave it to the Franciscans in 1482. The revolution ended the activities of the chapter but the 17th

Tautavel: Caune de l'Arago

Tautavel Museum: "the Neandertal Man"

century bell-tower shaped like a lantern-tower, is a reminder of it. To the north of Saint-Paul-de-Fenouillet the Agly and its tributary the Verdouble have dug out in a last buttress of the Corbières, the Galamus Gorges. The Agly, which has its source on the flanks of Bugarach Peak, drops down two hundred metres between entering and leaving the gorges over a distance of about five kilometres. It was in 1890 that a road was built here, mid-cliff, overhanging in places the bottom of the gorge by almost five hundred metres. A Spanish builder, a certain Ventura, and seven workers carried out this titanic work which meant digging out an access tunnel.

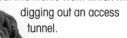

Peyrepertuse

Nature has powerfully protected this exceptional site. This formidable rocky ridge, which looks like a ship's hull, stretches over nearly three hundred metres from east to west and is a maximum of seventy metres wide. It ends, to the west, at the *prow* where San Jordi Castle rises up at an altitude of eight hundred metres. The site was occupied in ancient times and this goes back to the Romans. The first mention of the pagus of *Petre Pertuse* was in 842 in the charter established by Charles the Bald in favour of Milon. This name is said to be due to the existance of a pierced rock which was destroyed during work in 1250. Bernard, Count of Besalù's will of 1021 confirms the existence of the *castellum of Petrapertusa*, fiefdom of the Peyrepertuse family who, at the end of the 12th century were vassals of the viscount of Fenouillet who was himself vassal to the viscount of Narbonne who paid homage to the Count of Barcelona who became King of Aragon in 1162. This vassal link with the crown of Aragon allowed Peyrepertuse Castle to enjoy a relative immunity at the beginning of the crusade against the Albigensians. In 1217, Guillaume de Peyrepertuse had to surrender to Montfort, becoming his vassal in the presence of the Viscount of Narbonne. However this allegiance was short-lived because he was excommunicated in 1224 and in 1229 he was still resisting behind the ramparts of Puilaurens. His castle sheltered Cathars and *faidits* until 1240. The attempt by Trencavel to reconquer his lands had just failed at Carcassonne and Jean de Beaumont, at the head of the royal army, pushed home his advantage besieging Peyrepertuse which surrendered after three days of siege on 16 November 1240. This lower castle is the original Peyrepertuse Castle which occupies the east part of the rocky ridge. The surrender of the fortress in 1240 made it become a part of the defenses of the Pyrenean border. It was under the reign of Philip the Bold that San Jordi Castle, as well as the staircase carved out of the rock which led to it, were built. An esplanade protected by curtain walls thus makes up a fortified base whose surface area was equal to that of the town of Carcassonne. The Treaty of the Pyrenees in 1659 marked the end of the glorious era of Peyrepertuse even if a garrison was maintained there until the French Revolution.

The castle seems inaccessible. A small path leads as far as the barbican and follows the foot of the north curtain walls of the lower castle, flanked with two semi-circular towers. The inner courtyard is only accessible after crossing a small entrance door protected by double arrow slits. The access path passes through a passage just wide enough for one person. The courtyard is long and narrow. On the southern flank, the body of the building had a sink and toilets. On the south-west corner of the courtyard the old keep is made up

The five sons of Carcassonne

After the failure of Trencavel before the ramparts of Carcassonne in 1240, the fortress was considerably reinforced by the Capetians who sent royal representatives to establish themselves in the Castle of the Counts. Five castles, "the five sons of Carcassonne" formed an impressive first line of defence in front of the nearby Catalan-Aragon border: Aguilar, Quéribus, Peyrepertuse, Puilaurens and Termes. In 1659, the Treaty of the Pyrenees, signed in the Basque Country on the Isle of Pheasants in the waters of the Bidassoa and sealed by the marriage of Louis XIV and the Infanta Maria-Teresa, daughter of Philip IV, fixed the frontier between the two countries as the summit line of the Pyrenees, and definitively took away any strategic importance from these castles.

of two parallel buildings, Saint Mary's Church, mentioned in 1115 in a donation to the priory of Serrabone and the governor's accommodation, flanked to the west by a round tower which housed the cistern. Two curtain walls link the two buildings forming an almost perfect parallelogram and surrounding the courtyard called "shirt".

Between the lower castle and San Jordi Castle, the central wall becomes wider up to the far ends of the cliffs. Few parts remain and one's attention is immediately drawn to another building on the narrow promontory: San Jordi Castle. Its access stairway, the Saint Louis Stairway, with its sixty steps, seems to have been built intentionally above an impressively sheer cliff and when the place is beaten by gusts of wind, it is best to hold on tightly to the handrail. The eastern part includes a chapel and a keep while to the west San Jordi Rock rises up. Climbing up to San Jordi has to be attained, but once there, what an extraordinary view!

Peyrepertuse Castle: Saint Mary's Chapel

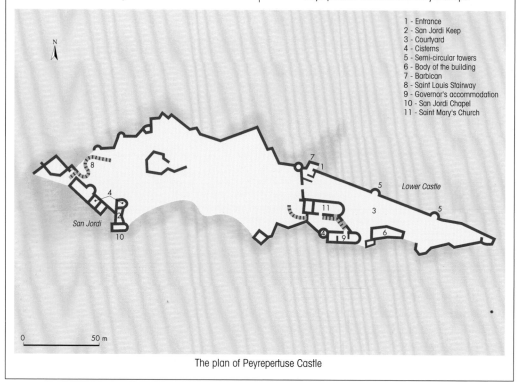

1 - Entrance
2 - San Jordi Keep
3 - Courtyard
4 - Cisterns
5 - Semi-circular towers
6 - Body of the building
7 - Barbican
8 - Saint Louis Stairway
9 - Governor's accommodation
10 - San Jordi Chapel
11 - Saint Mary's Church

Lower Castle

San Jordi

0   50 m

The plan of Peyrepertuse Castle

Quéribus

At the southern boundary of the Corbières, about three kilometres from the village of Cucugnan dear to Achille Mir, Quéribus Castle tops a rocky peak which is 728 metres high. It thus controls Grau de Maury pass and overlooks the Roussillon Plain. The viewpoint that it offers from its ramparts includes Peyrepertuse to the north-west and stretches as far as the sea to the south-east and to the Canigou to the south. The shape of the land lent itself to the building of a *castellum* of which the first mention was made in 1020 in the will of the Count of Besalù where Quéribus appears under the name of *Cherbucio*. The etymology of this name is difficult to establish but could mean "inhabited place on the rock". One century later, Quéribus became a dependence of the Count of Barcelona and then, after the marriage in 1137 between the Count of Barcelona, Raymond Bérenger IV and the heiress of the King of Aragon, passed to her. During the crusade against the Albigensians, Quéribus was not implicated but Fenouillèdes and Perapertusès were sanctuaries of many *faidit* lords and Cathars. In 1233, Benoît de Termes, Cathar bishop of Razès was in Quéribus and died there in 1241. Two years after the fall of Montségur, in 1246, a Cathar *parfait* Pierre Paraire and a few believers were living there. Chabert de Barbaira, a follower of Viscount Pierre de Fenouillet who died in 1242, commanded the place. In May 1255, the Seneschal of Carcassonne, Pierre d'Auteil, with the support of the archbishop of Narbonne, undertook the siege of Quéribus, the last bastion of Occitan resistance, which surrendered three weeks later. This quick surrender is probably explained by the fact that Chabert de Barbaira was no longer in the castle. He is said to have been first taken prisoner in early March 1255 near Carcassonne by Olivier de Termes, one of his former companions in arms, who had rallied

Not a soul from Cucugnan…

Achille Mir was born in 1822 in Escales between Carcassonne and Narbonne. First a school teacher, he resigned from public teaching to concentrate on his poetic work in French and then in Occitan, after joining the Félibrige, a Provençal literary school created in 1854 by seven Provençal poets including Frédéric Mistral, to defend the Provençal language and the Occitan languages. It was in 1884 that Achille Mir wrote *Loi sermou dal curat de Cucugna*, on a theme which had been developed by Roumanille, one of the seven founders of the school in Provençal and translated by Alphonse Daudet. He brought to this work all his verve and truculence that Henri Gougaud, who adapted the text into French, has been able to convey in the tiny theatre at the very heart of the village of Cucugnan. In about twenty minutes, the spectator is surrounded all at once by the text read by the storyteller and by the projected images which are added to by special effects. The story has a moral because: "as has been said, each one washed his own clothes; And since then Our Lord keeps / the people of Cucugnan from harm / Who live happily with peace in their souls / And thousands of times happier / Since they became pious."

Cucugnan

to the side of Louis IX. Quéribus then became a royal fortress at the southern frontier of the kingdom such as it was defined by the treaty of Corbeil in 1258 and was the object of great works which reinforced its defences. The present shape of the castle is probably the result of work carried out at the end of the 16th century under the authority of the states of Languedoc. Three walls fitted together follow the shape of the peak which seems to lengthen the keep. Its walls are up to four or even five metres thick; they have no openings on the east, west and north sides, that is the sides which give onto the exterior. The vault of the Pillar chamber rests on a single pillar which opens out into eight main ribs and four smaller ribs. This room was probably Saint Louis' Chapel. However, the date of its construction has not been formally established. In any case, it is not out of the question that it was built at an earlier date than the occupation of the castle by the Cathars.

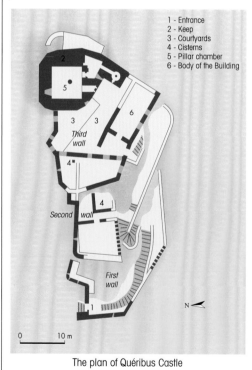

1 - Entrance
2 - Keep
3 - Courtyards
4 - Cisterns
5 - Pillar chamber
6 - Body of the Building

The plan of Quéribus Castle

A lion of combat

Chabert de Barbaira was a protector of the Cathars and probably a convinced heretic believer. He was also a warrior without equal who fought countless times against the French. As early as November 1209, he participated in the taking of Miramont Castle, on Alaric Mountain near Carcassonne, above a village which bears the name of Barbaira. He defended Toulouse in 1218 and was at the side of the future Raymond VII at the battle of Baziège in 1219. Between times he had participated in the conquest of Majorca with James I of Aragon. In 1240, he accompanied Trencavel in his attempt to reconquer and occupy Padern, property of Lagrasse Abbey, which, on the Verdouble Gorges, controlled access to Quéribus. After the fall of Quéribus, Chabert, this "lion of combat" was freed and spent the rest of his days in Roussillon.

Padern Castle

Fontfroide

In 1093, Aymeri I, Viscount of Narbonne, authorized Benedictine monks to establish themselves in a valley in the Corbières where a torrent fed by the *Fons frigidus* flowed. In 1144, the community became attached to Grandselve Abbey. One year later, when Bernard de Clairvaux went there, Grandselve became affiliated to the Order of Cîteaux and in 1146, Fontfroide in turn became Cistercian. Thanks to gifts from lords, the property of the abbey grew: in the 13th century it possessed twenty-five barns. In 1203 Pope Innocent III named two of its monks, Raoul and Pierre de Castelnau as legates with the mission of eliminating the heresy and in the heart of Cathar country, Fontfroide became a veritable citadel of the Catholic orthodox church. In 1297, Arnaud Nouvel was elected abbot. He was promoted to cardinal in 1310 and was a papal legate in England at the trial of the Templar dignitaries. At his death in 1317, he was, according to his wishes, buried in Fontfroide. His nephew, Jacques Fournier, succeeded him in 1311. Bishop of Pamiers in 1317, he conducted the tribunal of the Inquisition during the trial of the Cathars of Sabarthès. In December 1334, he became Pope in Avignon under the name of Benedict XII. The abbey is a marvellous example of Cistercian architecture. The lay brothers, religious but not monks dealt with material tasks, had their own refectory, a chamber with an ogive ribbed vault. From the abbey church, built in the second half of the 12th century, a staircase leads to the monks' dormitory. The Gothic cloister was built after the end of the 12th century and finished in the 14th century. Galleries are open on the garden side with arcades supported by geminated small columns, with capitals decorated with leaves. The passage from the east gallery of the cloister to the capitular chamber is through a semi-circular arch framed by two bays. Above the north gallery is a covered walk leading to the lay brothers' dormitory, covered with a barrel vault.

Cistercians and heretics

Bernard de Clairvaux had, as early as 1145, shown an example in the fight against heresy. In 1178, 1179 and 1181, Henri de Marcy, abbot of Cîteaux, went on a pastoral mission in the Toulouse area. In 1198, Innocent III, alerted to the strength of the heresy by the bishop of Auch, rushed the legates Rainier and Guy, both Cistercians, to the scene. In 1203, he added two other monks from Fontfroide to the legation, Pierre de Castelnau and Raoul. In 1204 they were present at the pleading of Carcassonne, organized by Peter II of Aragon. On 31 May 1204, Innocent III addressed an elegy to his two legates, which spread through the whole Cistercian Order, and named at their side a new legate, Arnaud-Amaury, abbot of Cîteaux, former abbot of Poblet and Grandselve, respectively daughter and mother abbey to Fontfroide. Foulque, abbot of Thoronet, had just been named bishop of Toulouse – he remained so for twenty-five years. In Montpellier in June 1206, Cistercian legates met Diègue and Dominic. Together they participated in conferences in Verfeil, Montréal and Pamiers where twelve Cistercian abbots including Guy, abbot of Les Vaux-de-Cernay, brought their contribution to the Holy preaching. Pierre de Castelnau was assassinated on the banks of the Rhône on 14 January 1208 and Arnaud-Amaury became the spiritual leader of the crusade against the Albigensians. In 1212, Arnaud-Amaury was named archbishop of Narbonne and Guy des Vaux-de-Cernay bishop of Carcassonne. In 1229, the abbot of Grandselve, Elie Garin, participated in preparing the Treaty of Meaux. From 1318 to 1325, Jacques Fournier, former abbot of Fontfroide, future pope as Benedict XII, led the interrogation of the heretics of Sabathès, in Montaillou, the "Occitan village" of the historian Emmanuel Le Roy Ladurie.

❶

❷

Lagrasse

The charter of the founding of Lagrasse Abbey, in the Orbieu Valley was before the year 800. Legend tells that it was Charlemagne himself, en route for the Iberian peninsula where he would fight the Moors who, passing a hermitage that he had here, founded a monastery. Many donations contributed to the development and prosperity of the abbey, which was dedicated to Mary. Around 1070, Lagrasse became the dependence of the Count of Barcelona, Raymond-Bérenger I and was attached to Saint Victor's of Marseilles. At the end of the 11th century and beginning of the 12th century, many abbeys, and not the least, became attached to it: in the area those of Saint-Polycarpe and Saint-Martin-des-Puits, and in Catalonia Saint-André de Sorède, Saint Martin du Canigou, Sant Pere de Galligants, San Feliú de Guixols. In 1224, Benoît d'Alignan became abbot of Lagrasse, in the same year as Amaury de Montfort abandoned Carcassonne, giving his land to the King of France. In 1226, Louis VIII started the Royal Crusade and the towns of the Midi such as Béziers and Carcassonne, duly encouraged by the abbot of Lagrasse surrendered to the Capetian without a fight.

The abbey is situated on the left bank of the Orbieu while the fortified village with the Plaisance Tower to the south, occupies the right bank. The two banks are joined, apart from the modern bridge, by a 12th century bridge and a ford. The tower belfry, which was erected by the abbot Philippe de Lévis in the early 16th century, overlooks all the buildings of the abbey and flanks the South transept and is forty-two metres high. It could have been eighty metres if the arrow which was to top it had been completed; the arms of the bishop of Mirepoix are carved on the east façade. The south arm of the transept with its three small apses, dates from the 11th century. The base of the tower which tops the north arm of the

transept is pre-Romanesque and is the oldest part of the abbey with the 6th century sarcophagus cover which is exhibited in the lapidary museum in the south lateral chapel. The abbey church, from the end of the 13th century, was built under the abbatiat of Auger de Gogenx whose arms, two blue and red triangles, are carved on a keystone while others have the arms of the abbey, the village of Lagrasse or the royal fleur-de-lis. Saint Bartholomew's Chapel dates from the same period, and the floor is covered in varnished terracotta tiles. The majority of the abbey buildings, attributed to abbot Bazin de Bezons, date from after 1745, while the cloister is from 1760. In 1989, the door giving access to the 13th century dormitory which had been walled up was re-opened and inside a carved Romanesque capital was found said to be the work of the master of Cabestany. He also worked on the main doorway of the abbey of which unfortunately only a few parts remain, in particular some voussoirs which have been scattered.

Saint-Martin-des-Puits

To the south-west of Lagrasse, at the foot of the Lacamp Plateau, Saint-Martin-des-Puits, originally a Carolingian monastery, became in 1093 a priory of Lagrasse Abbey. The choir, with a square apse, is pre-Romanesque. It communicates with the nave via an arch resting on marble columns. These columns are said to come from an ancient construction and are topped with two capitals, carved with acantha of Merovingian origin. The choir was surrounded by two opposite chapels in the 11th century which form the transept; the north chapel has been destroyed. The nave was also rebuilt in the 11th century. On the south and east walls of the choir are wall paintings dating from the early 12th century, showing fantastic animals, an Annunciation, Nebuchadnezzar, and the Three Hebrews.

Villerouge-Termenès

Villerouge-Termenès Castle rises above the village houses. It belonged to the archbishops of Narbonne who renovated it in the second half of the 13th century. In 1306, a village shepherd had been killed, during an argument, by a certain Guillaume Bélibaste who had taken flight. In 1309, the same Bélibaste had become a *parfait*, been arrested and imprisoned in the *Mur* of Carcassonne from where he escaped. He fled to exile and rejoined the Cathars of Sabarthès in Catalonia. He worked as a weaver and as a cobbler in Lérida, Tortosa, San Mateo and Morella. When in 1316 another *parfait*, Raymond de Toulouse died, he who was called "Mister Tortosa" became in fact the last Occitan *parfait*, as one of his equals, Raymond d'Alayrac, had been arrested. Bélibaste was captured in 1321 after being denounced. He died, burnt alive, in Villerouge-Termenès.

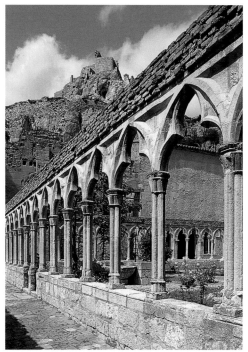

The cloister and the citadel, Morella

A very medieval setting

Mainly built in the 13th century, Villerouge-Termenès Castle with its four corners and crenellated round towers is a fine example of the medieval fortified castle. Its chambers, staircases and towers are the setting for a permanent audio-visual show which brings back to life "The world of Guilhem Bélibaste". Each year, during the "medieval summer festival" the inhabitants of the village make a reconstitution of the life of those who, six centuries ago, preceded them inside these walls. There is no doubt that good food was already appreciated as can be seen in the dishes served in the Medieval Rotisserie, prepared according to recipes of the times, forgotten but found again with the help of some historians. To taste them, no forks or plates are allowed. What, not at all! But spoons and knives, trenchers, cakes of unleavened bread or bowls with "ears". And to drink, goblets, jugs or goglets. In the Middle Ages, to lay a table was already an art…

Medieval Rotisserie: the banqueting hall

Termes

The lords of Termes were vassals of the Trencavels. Montfort had to make them surrender. The task was not easy because the castle seemed impregnable with its rocky peak protected to the north by the Terminet Gorges with the Sou river which joins the Orbieu near Durfort Castle, a possession of the lords of Termes and the home of the Durfort family, of which one member, the co-lord of Fanjeaux was a troubadour. Raymond de Termes was certainly elderly, but resolute, and was afraid "neither of God nor Men", as wrote Des Vaux-de-Cernay. The siege began in August 1210. On both sides, mangonels went into action. Occupying the advanced position of Le Termenet, the besieged were able to subject Simon de Montfort's troops to crossfire. However, as in Minerve, the besieged suffered from thirst. Termes was going to surrender when a storm refilled the stocks of water. However the badly maintained cisterns polluted the water. Dysentery ravaged the ranks of the defenders who fled during the night of 22 to 23 November. The siege had lasted three months. Raymond de Termes was captured and imprisoned in Carcassonne where he died in 1213. Termes became a royal fortress and was destroyed in the 17th century. A band of brigands occupied it and held the region to ransom from this impregnable hide-out. In order to eliminate these undesirable guests, the king decided to completely destroy the castle. The cost of the demolition work was 14 922 livres and ten sous. Only a few sections of the thick walls of this colossal construction remain. Two concentric walls must have surrounded the central keep flanked with a building which is difficult to identify but has retained, by the irony of fate, a façade with a window in the shape of a cross. This cross which seems to have been stencilled onto the blue of the sky is a reminder of the ferocious battles which, in the name of religion, spilled so much blood over the lands of Oc in the 13th century.

Olivier de Termes

After the taking of Termes Castle in August 1210, the son of Raymond de Termes, Olivier, saw the ranks of *faidit* lords, that is those who had been dispossessed of their land by the crusade, swell. Olivier participated in all the battles against the lords of the North and the King of France. He was with Trencavel in 1240. He surrendered a first time to Saint Louis in 1241 before participating in a coalition against him in 1242. He then rejoined him definitively in 1245. He therefore got back part of his property, including Aguilar Castle, but not Termes Castle. An ardent knight, he took part in the reconquest of Majorca beside James of Aragon. He accompanied Saint Louis to the crusades in 1248 and was at his bedside in Tunis when the king was carried off by the plague in 1270. According to some, this great warrior, who was probably never a heretic, died in the Holy Land on 12 August 1275; others think that, having died on his land, his remains rest in Fontfroide Abbey of which he was benefactor.

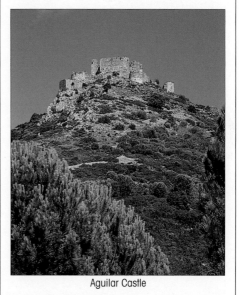

Aguilar Castle

Arques

At the beginning of the 11th century, Arques belonged to Lagrasse Abbey and a century later was passed into the hands of the lords of Termes. The *castrum* at that time did not yet possess a castle. In 1231, it was left to Pierre de Voisins, a former companion in arms to Simon de Montfort. Arques was part of the land that Olivier de Termes took back in 1246 after he surrendered to Louis IX. However he sold it in 1260 to its former occupant Pierre de Voisins whose son Gilles I had the village rebuilt as a bastide in 1268 and undertook the building of the castle and its keep. Gilles II de Voisins continued the work which was completed around 1316. The architecture of the keep, twenty metres high and on three floors, proves that the criteria of comfort and elegance were taken into account in its design without by any means neglecting the strict defensive aspects. At the heart of the Razès area,

a region which after the council of Pieusse in 1226 became the see of a Cathar bishopric, Arques was directly implicated in the events of the time. In 1210, the village saw the crusaders on their way from Termes to Puivert when they were going to lay siege to Coustaussa Castle a mere ten kilometres away, to the west of Arques. Coustaussa was built in the 12th century by the Trencavel family above the Sals Valley to control the passage between the Corbières and the Aude Valley. In the early 14th century, Pierre Authié converted some inhabitants of Arques to Catharism including a certain Pierre Maury who gave evidence later before Jacques Fournier. After the arrest in 1305 of Jacques Authié, son of Pierre and himself a *parfait*, the Cathars of Arques asked Pope Clement V, who was then in Lyon, directly to be reconciled with the Church. In the village of Arques is the birthplace of Déodat Roché (1877-1978), one of the first historians of Catharism. Inside is a permanent exhibition on the Cathar theme.

Coustaussa Castle

The Razès Area: water, abbeys, mysteries, hats and dinosaurs

For a long time, the Razès area was famous for its curative waters. In Rennes-les-Bains, the Romans, lovers of spas, used the hot sulphured, calcium carbonated, chlorinated and radioactive waters of the Sals Valley as did Queen Blanche de Castille in the 12th century, who gave her name to the resort: "the Queen's Baths". The Sals is an tributary of the Aude and rejoins it in Couiza where the 16th century former castle of the Dukes de Joyeuse can be found. They fought with the Ligueurs and played an important role during the Wars of Religion. Anne de Joyeuse, known for being one of the favourites of Henri III, died in the battle of Coutras in 1587 in which he had engaged, at the head of royal troops against Henri de Navarre, the future Henri IV. Rennes-le-Château overlooks the Aude and Sals Valleys. This promontory, from where both the passage at the foot of the Pyrenees and the mountain itself can be watched, was inhabited by man from early times. The village perched above the plain was, during its history, both coveted and feared. Visigoths and then Templars are said to have invaded the place in turn. From then

Rennes-le-Château: Magdala Library-Tower

Rennes-le-Château: the stoup in the church

Couiza: the Castle of the Dukes de Joyeuse

on, the most amazing legends would feed upon all the rumours of history, and never checked, never proved: a treasure is said to be hidden there! It could have been no more than a dream, the souvenir of fabulous lost riches, but the strange story of Abbot Saunière suddenly led weight to the mystery. A priest, Abbot Saunière, is said to have found this treasure at the end of the 19th century as well as documents that were "so important as to change the face of the world". He shared his secret with his servant, Marie, but despite all attempts to make her speak, the faithful maid always refused to break her master's trust, even on her deathbed. According to rumour, the expensive building work undertaken by Abbot Saunière were largely paid for by this treasure. The restoration of the church, the strange Magdala Library-Tower well-equipped with books, the luxurious villa called Bethania, trips to far-off places and festivities given on his property… all this certainly cost a lot! The bishop of Carcassonne himself became concerned about it and called the abbot to provide accounts, which he was not able to do. Abbot Saunière was deprived of his sacerdotal powers and died a short while later. Since then, Rennes-le-Château has been the scene of strange practices. All wish to have their chance to find Abbot Saunière's treasure. People listen, use

probes and dig… but in vain. The small town of Espéraza can be proud of its two very different and very unique museums. The presence of dinosaurs seems to be proved in the area 160 million years ago. Thanks to the talents of the researchers of Dinosauria, these extraordinary giants are no longer reduced to phantom skeletons but are almost lifelike. In the 18th century, also in Espéraza, the "cloches" were shaped and polished which became hats, as shown in the Hat Museum. To the north of Couiza, the hot water springs of Alet-les-Bains were, like those at Rennes-les-Bains, discovered in Roman times. Only some parts of the church, the capitular chamber and the north entrance door remain from the former Carolingian abbey. Its destruction dates from the battles which stained the Razès area with blood during the Wars of Religion. It was, at the end of the 12th century, the scene of a sinister episode which proves that in Languedoc the relations between the local lords and the Church could be greatly conflicting. In 1197, Bertrand de Saissac was very dissatisfied that the abbot of Saint-Polycarpe had been elected as successor to Pons d'Amiel, abbot of Alet. He had the former imprisoned and had the latter exhumed. He organized a new and macabre election, presided over by the body which placed his own candidate at the head of the abbey.

Alet Abbey: the apse

Esperaza dinosaur Museum: reconstruction of a Dromaesaurus

105

Limoux, Notre-Dame de Marceille Chapel: the porch

Limoux: Saint Martin's Church

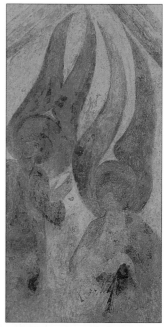

Saint-Polycarpe: a fresco from the former abbey church

Saint-Polycarpe

4

CARCASSÈS, CABARDÈS, MINERVOIS, BÉZIERS AND NARBONNE

Limoux and Saint-Polycarpe

Limoux, between the Languedoc plains and the Pyrenean mountains, used the waters of the Aude for a long time to develop a textile industry which has today disappeared. It still has the atmosphere of a medieval town, surrounded by ramparts. One round tower and sections of the curtain walls are the only remains of this formidable barrier which comprised nineteen of these towers. Saint Martin's Church main doorway and columns are Romanesque but its nave and ambulatory are Gothic; its furnishings are much later and its finely carved octagonal bell-tower dates from the 16th century. Due to its position, the town could not remain aloof from events linked to the crusade against the Albigensians: it was taken, as early as 1209 by Simon de Montfort who gave it to one of his vassals, Lambert de Thury and in Pieusse a great Cathar council was held in 1226.

One kilometre from the town, Notre-Dame de Centeilles, place of pilgrimage, houses a black madonna.

Saint-Polycarpe Abbey stands in a valley through which the Saint-Polycarpe river flows, a tributary of the Aude which it rejoins upstream of Limoux. Founded in 780 by Attala, a Spaniard fleeing the Moors, with the help of the Carolingians, it was attached to Lagrasse Abbey and then to Alet before recovering its independence. Only the 11th century church has resisted the ravages of time. The vaults of its single nave are decorated with 12th century paintings representing scenes from the Apocalypse. The side chapels house two 10th century Carolingian altars. 14th century head reliquaries of Saints Polycarpe and Benedict as well as a silver monstrance from the same era, are exhibited here.

Blanquette and carnival

According to legend, the monks of Saint-Hilaire discovered in the 16th century the principle of the first natural sparkling wine, Blanquette de Limoux. The area of the *appellation contrôlée* is made up of forty-one villages. Three white grape varieties, Mauzac, Chardonnay and Chenin, are included in Blanquette as they are in Crémant de Limoux which received the appellation in 1990. In Limoux, wine and festivities go well together. Limoux has its carnival. Sundays in winter from January to March, sometimes on Saturdays and for Shrove Tuesday, three sessions are organized at 11am, 5pm and 10pm. To the rhythm of the *fécos*, the *masques* followed by fifteen musicians go from one café to the other. The morning excursion is based on the grotesque whereas the afternoon excursion is organized around Pierrot holding his *carabène* and the night excursion by the light of the *entorches* is the most spectacular. On the last day, the guy is judged and burnt, watched by the *masques* and the *badauds* or jesters who, to celebrate the event, go through the mad night of Blanquette together.

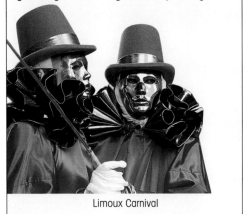

Limoux Carnival

Saint-Hilaire

It was in the 6th century that, according to legend, Saint Hilaire had an oratory built on a hill at the foot of which flowed the Lauquet, a tributary of the Aude. At the end of the 8th century, an abbey was founded in this place and the chapel gave way to the abbey church. The monastic establishment was, first of all, dedicated to Saint Saturnin. However, after the relics of Saint Hilaire were discovered on 22 February 970 and in the presence of Garin, the abbot of Saint-Michel de Cuxa, the abbey passed into the holy patronage of the first bishop of Carcassonne. Roger I, Count of Carcassonne and his wife Adélaïde, great benefactors of the abbey which had opted for the Benedictine rule, were interred there in 1012. The abbey church, which can still be seen today, dates from the end of the 12th century. It still has, in the south apse, a 12th century sarcophagus in white Pyrenees marble. It was certainly made by the Master of Cabestany who, in several scenes narrates the arrest and martyrdom, tied by feet and hands to a furious bull in 250 a.d. and the laying-out by Saint Puelles of Saint Sernin or Saint Saturnin, who evangelized Languedoc and was the first bishop of Toulouse. The artist has carefully reproduced the impetuous bull, with fettered back hooves, while Saint Saturnin blesses with open hand his tormentors and the spectators. This sarcophagus was the main altar of the abbey church but it was only later, between 1345 and 1645 that it received the relics of Saint Hilaire. The abbey has preserved a large number of the monastery buildings which surround the Gothic cloister, in trapezoid shape, built in the 14th century. The geminated columns are topped with double capitals carved with leaves and monsters. Opening onto the southern gallery is the refectory: the reading chair, in stone, is fixed into the wall. The reader carried out *lectio divina* to the monks who ate in silence.

The Master of Cabestany

This sculptor worked during the third quarter of the 12th century in Tuscany, at the abbey church of Sant'Antimo where a capital shows Daniel in the lions' den, in San Giovanni Church in Sugana, in Navarre in Errondo, but above all in the Languedoc and in Catalonia. The Master worked, with his chisel, apart from the Saint-Hilaire sarcophagus, the capital of the Assumption in Rieux-Minervois Church, the main doorway of Lagrasse Abbey, the sculptures in the apse of Saint-Papoul, the west door of Sant Pere de Rodes Abbey, the cornice of the tympanum of Boulou Church and the tympanum preserved in Cabestany Church near Perpignan, one of his masterpieces, and which gave the name to this artist with such original and powerful talent but who was completely anonymous. Works of the master or of his atelier? It is difficult to be sure, but all present the same dominant characteristics: individuals with disproportionate hands and feet, long fingers, wide open eyes. The master had an acute sense of setting a scene and used a process of carving on two pieces which fitted together to give relief to compositions where an obvious interest in perspective is clearly visible.

The tympanum of Cabestany Church

Carcassonne

At the foot of the Black Mountain, where the Aude, coming from the Razès, to the south, changes direction and goes on towards the Mediterranean, Carcassonne has always had a strategic position. It was in the 3rd century b.c. that the Volques Tectosages occupied the hill of the present town, the oppidum of *Carcaso*. In 118 b.c., the Narbonne area was founded, *pax Romana* reigned and Carcassonne – it was already called this – prospered. Before the barbarian threat, in the 3rd century, it surrounded itself with ramparts from which about thirty towers soared upwards. In the 5th century the Visigoths installed themselves. At the beginning of the 8th century, the Saracens took it and were then chased away by Pepin the Short. The legend of Lady Carcass had its origin in these events. The besieged town was held by the Moors. The Moor king was killed in action and the provisions were running out. Lady Carcass, the wife of the dead king, had a sow stuffed with wheat thrown to the foot of the ramparts, thus giving the impression that the town still had plenty of reserves to the Franks who then lifted the siege. It was in the 11th century that Bernard Aton Trencavel became Viscount of Béziers and of Carcassonne. A fresco of Castle of the Counts shows the viscount in combat against the Moors in Spain in 1118. His dynasty cleverly played with the rivalries between the Houses of Toulouse and Aragon and, in the 12th century, had the Castle of the Counts built at the western end of the Lower-Empire wall which still made up the main part of the fortifications of Carcassonne. During the same 12th century, Catharism spread in Occitan lands. The worst could still be avoided in 1204 when a meeting between Cathars and Catholics took place at Carcassonne in the presence of Peter II of Aragon. However, in early August 1209, the ost crusaders took Carcassonne. Montfort became the head of the crusade and received

The destiny of the Trencavels

In the 10th and 11th centuries, the Trencavels possessed the Viscounties of Albi, Nîmes, Béziers, Agde and Carcassonne. They often had passionate relations with the House of Toulouse. Their fate was often violent if not tragic. In 1153, Viscount Raymond was made a prisoner by Raymond V who freed him in 1154 against guarantees. He was assassinated in 1167 "by a bourgeois of the town" in La Madeleine Church in Béziers, the same place where seven thousand inhabitants of Béziers would die, forty-two years later at the tragic turning-point in the sacking of Béziers by the crusaders. His son, Roger avenged him and married Azalaïs in 1171, daughter of Raymond V of Toulouse. The Cathar sympathies of his son Raymond-Roger gave the barons of the north who had started a crusade in answer to the call of Innocent III, a pretext to take Béziers and the town of Carcassonne, where the young Viscount had withdrawn, in 1209. Made a prisoner, Raymond-Roger died on 10 November 1209 in the jails of Carcassonne, of dysentery according to some, assassinated according to others. His son lived in exile at the court of the King of Aragon but in 1240 tried, with the help of other *faidit* lords, to reconquer the lands of his fathers, but failed before the walls of Carcassonne and had to go back into exile.

Béziers: the Trencavel seal

Trencavel's fiefdom. The son of the latter, Raymond, came back to Carcassonne in 1224 but the Royal Crusade of Louis VIII hunted him down in 1226. In a last attempt to reconquer his land in 1240, he took Montolieu and Saissac but failed before Carcassonne. Louis IX then reinforced the fortifications of the Cité and authorized the building of a bastide on the left bank of the Aude; Philip the Bold and Philip the Fair built the outer wall. Immediately, Carcassonne played a role of stronghold in the south of the kingdom and in 1355 the Black Prince, although he set fire to the bastide, did not dare attack the fortress which, after the signature of the Treaty of the Pyrenees in 1659 lost all military value and was subjected to the ravages of time. In the 19th century, Prosper Mérimée, Cros-Mayrevieille and Viollet-le-Duc were the promoters of its restoration.

The ramparts of Carcassonne are made up of two concentric walls giving the limits of the palisades. At the summit of the ramparts is a

Carcassonne: the Bishop's Tower

The Castle of the Counts

A fortress within a fortress, the castle of Carcassonne dates from the 12th and 13th centuries but was built on even older remains as is shown by traces of human occupation in the part which is attached to the back of the Gallo-Roman wall. Rebuilt during the Middle Ages, the Castle of the Counts is an enormous rectangular construction surrounded by a dry moat and protected by a semi-circular barbican. The principle of this enormous building, flanked with towers and protected by the rounded shield of the barbican rested on the simple idea that it should be able to hold for a long time even if the town had already fallen into the hands of an enemy. Of course the whole edifice was surrounded by wooden defences, "hourds", hanging from the tops of the walls, brattices and high palisades. However, these were only short-term palliatives because assailants easily overcame these rather derisory obstacles with fire. The most surprising element was the method of obstructing enemies with complicated passages, strange detours which brought them into the range of the defenders' arrows. The building itself included two large detached buildings and two courtyards. The Lapidary Museum, housed in the rooms of the Castle of the Counts presents an important collection of remains coming from the town and the region. The rooms have been organized in chronological order, from Ancient times with Roman milestones and Gallo-Roman remains, and go on through the Middle Ages with Merovingian and Carolingian sarcophagi and their carved capitals, modillions and elaborate corbels mainly coming from buildings in the town. A beautiful 13th century recumbent effigy in sandstone represents the mortal remains of a knight and is exhibited in the so-called recumbent effigy room.

widow's walk protected by merlons and battlements and lined with "hourds", wooden platforms overlooking the outer walls of the ramparts. The two walls are flanked with towers. Thirteen towers are spread along the outer rampart and twenty-six along the inner wall. On the inner rampart are: the Tréseau Tower, to the north-east, a building with vaulted rooms with Gothic style windows; the Tower of Justice is a round tower reinforced under Saint Louis, which had already been used as a refuge by the viscounts Trencavel when the city was attacked by the crusaders; the Tower of the Inquisition was, as its name implies, the seat of the Inquisition; the square Bishop's Tower built astride the palisade, blocked any communication between the north and south ramparts; the postern of Saint-Nazaire Tower was only accessible by ladder which could be removed in case of danger: this tower must have protected the Saint-Nazaire basilica just behind it. Outside the outer wall, Vade Tower is a cylinder of five floors where toilets, a well

and a chimney were built. Some towers are *open at the throat*: open on the inside, they form a half-circle jutting out on the outside of the ramparts and could not be used as a stronghold by enemies who might have occupied them. The ramparts have been rebuilt over the years using various materials. Near the Avar Tower, enormous stones from the Roman wall are still visible at the base of the walls: above, layers of bricks and roughstone were added in the 4th and 5th centuries. Finally, at the time of the first Viscounts of Carcassonne, the town saw its girdle of walls reinforced by the raising of the curtain walls supported by worked stones, smooth and regular and topped with merlons and crenellations. All the architectural elements of defence known at the time were used in Carcassonne: inaccessible watch-towers, posterns and loopholes which had to reinforce the weakest points of the fortress, i.e. access points, "hourds" and machicolations which were very useful for throwing many projec-

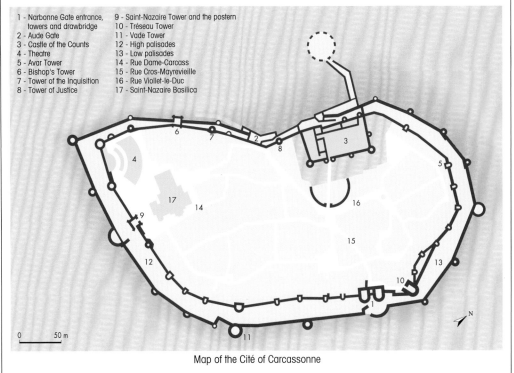

1 - Narbonne Gate entrance, towers and drawbridge
2 - Aude Gate
3 - Castle of the Counts
4 - Theatre
5 - Avar Tower
6 - Bishop's Tower
7 - Tower of the Inquisition
8 - Tower of Justice
9 - Saint-Nazaire Tower and the postern
10 - Tréseau Tower
11 - Vade Tower
12 - High palisades
13 - Low palisades
14 - Rue Dame-Carcass
15 - Rue Cros-Mayrevieille
16 - Rue Viollet-le-Duc
17 - Saint-Nazaire Basilica

0   50 m

Map of the Cité of Carcassonne

tiles onto assailants, arrow-slits and loop-holes. Narbonne Gate is the main gate to the town. It is surrounded by two buttressed towers. A small castle and a barbican complete its defences, protecting one of the rare access points to the interior of the town. Aude Gate, also powerfully fortified by a barbican, a small castle and an enormous machicolation dominates an access ramp edged with walls. The Castle of the Counts itself, reinforced by a deep moat and a barbican became a citadel within a citadel.

The building of Saint-Nazaire Basilica is said to have begun at the end of the 11th century and Pope Urban II, the same who had preached in 1095 in Clermont for the first crusade in the Holy Land, blessed the first stone. However the work was only completed in the mid-14th century. The nave is the oldest part of the building. Its very sober Romanesque full arch is in contrast with the Gothic apse with six radiating chapels decorated with stained-glass windows. The oldest, from the 14th century, show scenes from the Old and New Testaments. The other stained-glass windows date from the 16th and 17th centuries. Light also filters through the rose-windows of the transept. Statues arranged on the top of the pillars in the nave are topped with small canopies in stone lacework: the most remarkable are those of the Virgin and Child. Guy des Vaux-de-Cernay, brother of Pierre, the chronicler of *Hystoria Albigensis*, was bishop of Carcassonne in 1215. He had the refectory, cellars and stables rebuilt as they had been destroyed during the first battles of the crusade. These parts have disappeared today. In the mid-13th century, bishop Guilhem Radulphe had an infirmary and a chapel built which became at his death his own funerary chapel; a sarcophagus is topped with a statue of the bishop. Work in the 14th century was the work of bishops Pierre de Rochefort and Pierre Rodier. The first lies in rest there in a tomb with a recumbent effigy. As for the pink marble paving stone with an effigy of a knight

in armour decorated with Toulouse crosses and lions, it only dates from the 19th century. The town has preserved its medieval aspect: narrow and winding streets, half-timbered façades and small open squares around wells. By royal order, the two villages attached to the first wall, Saint-Vincent and Saint-Michel, were destroyed, as their loyalty to their immediate suzerain, the Viscount of Carcassonne was fatal to them. Even after the royal pardon of 1247, they were not rebuilt. However, Saint Louis authorized the founding of the lower town which took full advantage of its position as a suburb outside the walls to develop trading activities. This bastide has all the characteristics of new towns built in the Middle Ages, a chessboard design, dominated by Saint Vincent's Church tower, a central square, a city wall which no longer exists and a moat which is now transformed into boulevards. It was in one of these houses at the centre of the Saint-Louis bastide that Joë Bousquet lived paralysed from 1918 to 1950.

"There is a night within a night..."

Joë Bousquet was born in Narbonne in 1897. After having enlisted before the date of his military service, the most decorated man in his regiment, Bousquet was wounded in the Battle of Vailly in 1918. He remained paralysed and lived the rest of his days in a room of N°53, Rue de Verdun in Carcassonne, which became a literary salon frequented by painters, writers, poets and philosophers such as Paul Valéry, Max Ernst, René Magritte, Louis Aragon, André Gide and Dali. But behind these closed shutters, calming his pain with an opium pipe, the poet took from his misfortune the strength which allowed him to build another life "to only feel grace and gift" and also his inspiration. And like a flower which grows from a land of despair, a poetic work of prose sprang, first published by Jean Paulhan.

②

Saissac, Villelongue and Hautpoul

To the north-west of Carcassonne, on the south slopes of the Black Mountain, at the confluence of the Vernassonne and the Aiguebelle, Saissac stands on an abrupt peak carved out of the rock by the two streams. In 1209, when the castle was attacked by Bouchard de Marly, it was the fief of Bertrand de Saissac. This vassal of the Viscount of Béziers, Roger II, became, at the death of the latter in 1194, the guardian of Raymond-Roger Trencavel who was then aged nine and who would die in the jails of Carcassonne in 1209. In 1197, he brutally imposed his candidate on the Abbey of Alet. In 1240, Raymond-Roger Trencavel's son took back the castle for a short time which then went into the hands of Lambert de Thury and then the Lévis family and was almost completely rebuilt in the 14th and 15th centuries.

On the banks of the Vernassonne, monks who had come from Saissac founded Saint-Marie de Villelongue Abbey at the end of the 12th century. Like other Cistercian abbeys in the Languedoc, Villelongue, a few leagues from Saissac Castle whose lords were notorious Cathars, participated in the fight against the heresy. Its 14th century cloister of which only a gallery remains flanks to the south the imposing ruins of the abbey church dating from the 12th and 13th centuries, where the square apse can be noted, an architectural solution which was often used by the Cistercians. The 12th century capitular chamber has an ogived vault while the sacristy which is contemporary has barrel vaulting.

On the south slope of the Black Mountain, near Mazamet, Simon de Montfort invaded Hautpoul thanks to a thick fog on 11 April 1212. This castle, above the Arnette Gorges, impressed Pierre des Vaux-de-Cernay who described it as "built on the slope of a very high and very precipitous mountain on enormous almost inaccessible rocks".

Cabardès Caves

At the foot of the Nore Peak, the highest point of the Black Mountain at 1210 metres, nature has excavated vast cavities out of the limestone rock. The chambers of Limousis Cave extend over more than half a kilometre; the last of them has a formation of immaculate white aragonite, more than three metres in diameter. The Clamoux which passes through the village of Cabrespine is lost in the chasm. According to a legend, ducks are said to have been swallowed up in the depths of the underground river and come out again, alive, at the resurgence of Le Pestril, near Lastours. By colouring the water of the river, speleologists have reproduced this event. The *Chamber of the Giant Chasm, the Red Chambers and the Chamber of 7th Heaven* represent, other than impressive dimensions, a whole range of concretions: stalagmites, stalactites, fistulas and bushes of aragonite.

Cabrespine Chasm

Lastours

In the 11th century, the castles of Lastours were the fief of the lords of Cabaret, vassals of the Trencavels. Their ruins stand above the village of Lastours, on a rocky crest defined by the deep valley of the Grésilhou torrent to the west and of the Orbiel to the east. Of the four castles, Cabaret, the most northerly, Surdespine, the most southerly and Quertinheux existed in the early 13th century; Tour Régine was built near the two first around 1260. The lords received troubadours there such as Raymond de Miraval or Peire Vidal, who dedicated their verses to Brunissende and Loba, the Louve of Pennautier, both ladies of Cabaret; but also heretics. In autumn 1209, Montfort renounced a siege of Cabaret and shortly afterwards the Duke of Burgundy left for the North leaving Montfort with seriously reduced numbers. In 1210, Cabaret saw one hundred men arrive before its ramparts, with their eyes torn out, their noses and upper lips cut off, led by one of them who had only been blinded in one eye, the defenders of Bram who had been made to suffer this punishment by Montfort. In March 1211, after the fall of Termes, Pierre-Roger de Cabaret negotiated his surrender against the freedom of Bouchard de Marly, a close ally of Montfort, who he had made a prisoner in 1209 and who he freed "freshly bathed, hair well dressed, clothed and perched on a palfrey", according to Guillaume de Tudèle. In 1223, he retrieved his castle which sheltered Pierre Isarn, the Cathar bishop of Carcassonne until 1226 and became the most active resistance centre against the French led by Seneschal Imbert de Beaujeu. However after the council of Toulouse in 1229, the lords of Cabaret had to abandon their fief that they only recovered for a few weeks when they accompanied Trencavel in his attempt to reconquer in 1240. As for the *parfaits* and *faidits* that they found there, they took refuge in Montségur and in the Fenouillèdes area.

2 000 years of metallurgy

The Black Mountain is an ancient massif of Hercynian type whose underground is rich in minerals: iron, copper, lead, argentiferous lead and gold. The Romans mined the iron and established on the domain of the Forges of the Martys, a centre for iron metallurgy which functioned from the 1st century b.c. to the 3rd century a.d. During this period, more than thirty-seven thousand tonnes of iron were produced in these furnaces. It is probable that in the Middle Ages the lords of Cabaret founded a part of their wealth and power on the product of these iron deposits from the area that surrounded their castles and on the work of their forges. In the 15th and 16th centuries, silver was extracted from the veins of the mines in La Caunette. It was only in the 19th century that the gold deposits in Salsignes were exploited. A Museum of Mining and Metallurgy in the Black Mountain will soon see the light of day inside the Rabbier factory in Lastours.

Copper ore

Caunes-Minervois

The bishop of the Carcassès, Pierre Isarn lived in Cabaret as was witnessed by Raymond d'Aiffre later, in 1243: "I saw in Cabaret, in the diocese of Carcassonne, Pierre Isarn bishop of the heretics and his companions in their house, they were preaching there". At the end of the year 1226, Pierre Isarn left Cabaret. He reappeared in the Lauragais near Auriac. It was there that Imbert de Beaujeu, cousin of Louis VIII and supreme commander of the royal army captured the most active of the Cathar *parfaits*. Pierre Isarn was delivered into the hands of the archbishop of Narbonne. Condemnation fell, clear and without appeal: the pyre for a convinced heretic. The sentence was carried out in Caunes-Minervois, in the presence of King Louis VIII. It was Guiraud Abit, one of the companions of Pierre Isarn who succeeded him. This was in a Carolingian monastery which was built in several stages from the 11th to the 14th century, the abbey church of Caunes-Minervois, dedicated to Saint Peter and Saint Paul.

To the west of Caunes-Minervois, the church of Rieux-Minervois was built in the second half of the 12th century on the site of a primitive church dedicated to the Virgin. The new church, also consecrated to the mother of the Lord, has a central nave with seven sides surrounded by a deambulatory with fourteen sides. This rotunda shape unique in the Languedoc and which can be found in Neuvy-Saint-Sépulcre, in Saint-Bénigne de Dijon and also in Sainte-Marie de Planès church, in the Cerdagne and the Conflent, is known as the marial design. Fourteen capitals were carved by the famous Master of Cabestany. Other Romanesque buildings can be found in the Minervois area: the chapels of Notre-Dame de Centeilles and Saint-Germain-de-Cesseras, the church of Pouzols-Minervois whose apse, nave and the two first floors of the bell-tower date from the late 12th century or early 13th century.

Rieux-Minervois, Notre-Dame Church: a capital by the Master of Cabestany

1

2

Minerve

The Cesse and its tributary, the Brian, have cut out deep gorges which join in Minerve isolating and protecting a site which has always presented a strategic interest. On this natural mound, the lords of Minerve possessed a castle of which only a few rare remains can be seen such as the north buttress. This castle protected the access to the fortified village which clings to the side of the cliff. After the sacking of Béziers in July 1209, many Cathars took refuge in Minerve. A *faidit*, Guiraud de Pepieux, who had come from Puisserguier, hid out in Minerve at the end of 1209, where he mutilated two crusader knights who he had taken prisoner: he tore out their eyes and cut off their noses, ears and upper lips; five months later the defenders of Bram were subjected to the same mutilations. The crusaders started the siege of the village in June 1210. The shape of the land made the customary assault difficult, so Simon de Montfort installed four catapults on the edge of the cliffs. The village and the castle were subjected to incessant bombardments. There was much damage but above all the covered walkway which led to the only source of water was destroyed. This was very serious as it was very hot during the summer of 1210. Thirst had become the worst enemy of the besieged. Guillaume de Minerve had to surrender after five weeks of siege. The crusaders invaded the village to the chant of the *Te Deum*. The lord of Minerve lost his castle but was saved, as were his soldiers. As for the Cathars, they were asked to recant. One hundred and forty of them, the majority, refused. On 22 July, they threw themselves voluntarily onto the flames of a pyre that the crusaders had prepared in the Ravine of the Cesse. And the dove, a contemporary work by Jean-Luc Séverac, is a rendering of the representations of doves, of Cathar origin, found at Montségur and Ussat. And the fragment of the blue sky is also a symbol of peace.

Hurepel Museum

It is at the heart of Minerve, in one of the oldest houses in the village, that the creators of the Hurepel Museum have reconstituted the epic of the crusade against the Albigensians in Languedoc, by using hundreds of small figurines. The decor, always very carefully researched, the gestures and attitudes of the characters, their costumes and their arms, correspond to historical documents that have come to us and contribute much realism to the different scenes shown. Visiting the museum, which has commentaries in different languages, reminds us that the South saw, at the dawn of the 13th century, in the torment which broke out against these *bougres d'Albigeois*, the rapid and definitive disappearance of a civilisation in the Oc language which was refined and precious.

A 'parfait' being interrogated

Béziers

Béziers, standing on a rocky buttress, dominates the river Orb and, far off, the beautiful Hérault plain. The Volques, a tribe of Gauls, occupied the oppidum of *Baeterrae* near that of Ensérune as early as the 3rd century. Vines have always been the riches of the town. Pliny had already tasted the wine of this Roman colony founded in 36 b.c., in the 1st century a.d. The town then sacrificed to the imperial creed as shown by the statue of Pépézuc but was evangelized by Aphrodise in the 4th century. Tradition tells that the saint, decapitated by the Roman executioner, found his head at the bottom of a well and transported it himself to his own tomb. Béziers had to face barbarian assaults and then became a part of Septimania in 460. In 725 it was the Arab troops of Anbasa who invaded it before it was freed by the Franks of Pepin the Short. The fief of the Trencavels having been *exposed as prey*, Béziers suffered, on 22 July 1209, the sacking of the crusaders which ended in the massacre of seven thousand inhabitants who had taken refuge in the Church of La Madeleine. The city had other difficult times, from the Wars of Religion until the wine crisis of 1907, but took full advantage of the opening, in 1681 of the Canal of Two Seas, built by Pierre Paul de Riquet. The construction of Saint-Nazaire Cathedral was undertaken, in the 12th century, by Master Gervais. The cloister, which is next to it, was built in the 14th century and the bell-tower had to be rebuilt, having collapsed during Christmas night in 1354. Saint James' Church dates from the 10th century.

The Inquisition condemned the heretics who recanted to penances including pilgrimages: Notre-Dame-des-Grâces de Sérignan, on the banks of the Orb, downstream of Béziers, was the object of a *peregrinatio minor*, minor because it was nothing like the distances to be covered for the pilgrimages to Rome or Compostella.

The oppidum of Ensérune

The occupation of the site is ancient and goes back to the 6th century b.c. Greek and Etruscan influences are noted as early as the 5th century b.c. since ceramics which came from Attica and Campania have been found. Built on a chessboard pattern and protected by its ramparts, the town stretched to the summit of the oppidum. From 230 b.c. onwards, the town grew and the Roman influence became preponderant. Many archaeological remains such as silos, cisterns, and foundations of houses are preserved as much on the site itself as in Ensérune Museum where there are objects discovered during campaigns of excavations undertaken since 1915. The oppidum has overlooked Montady Lake, which dried up, now in radiating parcels of land since 1247.

A perfume burner

1

2

Narbonne

Many remains prove that Narbonne was already inhabited in Prehistoric times. Capital of Gallia Narbonensis, situated on the *Via Domitia*, it was from its port that the produce of Gaul was transported to Rome. Visigoths, Saracens and Carolingian Franks all took turns to inhabit the town.

During the crusade, Narbonne, learning the lesson from the tragedy of Béziers, surrendered to the ost. The town became a strategic point where the crusaders' armies arriving in the Midi through the Rhône Valley concentrated. It was during the Narbonne Conference in 1211 that Peter II of Aragon accepted the homage of Montfort, thus dispossessing his former vassals, the Trencavels; on the same occasion, he entrusted the education of his son Jacques, then aged three, to the military head of the crusade. His son's marriage to Amicie, Montfort's daughter was arranged. On 18 April 1214, it was in Narbonne that the Counts of Foix and Comminges surrendered to the legate Pierre de Bénévent who, in fact, convinced Montfort to release Jacques, the son of Peter II, who had been a hostage since the battle of Muret and who was demanded by the Aragon people. Between times, Arnaud-Amaury, the spiritual leader of the crusade had become bishop of Narbonne: in 1216 he excommunicated Montfort, his former ally, who wanted to take his titles.

From the medieval period the town has kept some exceptional monuments in the centre, near the Robine Canal, which connects the Canal du Midi to Port-la-Nouvelle by Bages and Sigean Lakes. The Archbishops' Palace was entered through Ancre Passage, between the Old Palace (Romanesque) and the New Palace (Gothic). It was flanked at its south-east corner by the Gilles-Aycelin Keep. The elegance of the Gothic Saint Just and Saint Pasteur's Cathedral is accentuated by the balance and harmony of the cloister at a corner of which stands the former bell-tower of the Carolingian church.

Amphoralis

To the north of Narbonne, near Sallèles-d'Aude, Gallo-Roman potters established their workshops. The clay soil, the plentiful supplies of water underground or brought by aqueduct from the Cesse, the wood necessary for the kilns, supplied by nearby forests, were all favourable to this situation. These potters baked in their fifteen kilns, as well as tiles, pottery, bricks, weighing scales and lamps, wine amphora which were filled with the fragile nectar produced by the vines of the region. A note painted on the neck indicated the nature of the contents: *picatum* for a dark wine, *passum* for a sweet liqueur-like wine, *mulsum* for a honeyed wine. It was two wine-growers who luckily discovered the archaeological site in 1968, which has been excavated since 1976 by a team of Government researchers. All activities have been identified from the extraction of clay, throwing, drying and baking in kilns capable of reaching temperatures of 950°C. In the site museum, under the great wings of the white butterfly, you can see all of this.

Sallèles-d'Aude, Amphoralis: kiln and amphora

INDEX

A

Agen 45, 57
Aguilar 83, 101
Albi 20, 48-49
Alet-les-Bains 104-105
Alzonne 26
Amphoralis 127
Ansignan (aqueduct) 84-85
Arques 81, 102-103
Aude Gorges 81
Auterive 41
Avignon 38-39
Avignonet 41-43, 57, 75, 79
Ax-les-Thermes 45, 73

B

Baziège 26, 39, 40
Beaucaire 34-35
Bédeilhac Cave 71
Bélesta 67, 84-85
Béziers 24, 111, 124-125
Biron 32
Bouan (fortified cave) 76-77
Bram 28-29, 51, 63, 119, 123
Bruniquel 26-27, 30

C-D

Cabardès 55, 117
Cabrespine Chasm 117
Cahors 16-17, 21, 30
Camon 66-67
Canal du Midi 8, 58-59
Carcassès 21, 23, 33, 39, 121
Carcassonne 14, 27, 38, 110-115
Casseneuil 25, 41
Castelnaud 34-35
Castelnaudary 30, 39, 49, 56-57
Castelsarrasin 40
Castres 22, 26, 30
Caudiès-de-Fenouillèdes 85
Caunes-Minervois 120-121
Chalabre 67, 79
Corbières 86-103
Cordes 50-51
Couiza 104-105
Coustaussa 103
Cucugnan 91
Durfort 101

E-F-G

Ensérune (oppidum) 125
Espéraza 105
Fanjeaux 18-19, 62-63
Fenouillèdes 84-85
Fenouillet 85
Foix 68-69
Fontestorbes Fountain 66-67
Fontfroide Abbey 94-95
Força Réal (hermitage) 85
Fou (clue de la) 85
Frau Gorges 66-67
Gaillac 30, 32
Galamus Gorges 84-85

H-L

Hautpoul 32, 116-117
Hurepel Museum 123
La Salvetat 36
La Vache Cave 71
Labécède-Lauragais 40
Labouiche (underground river) 73
Lagarde Castle 66-67
Lagrasse 96-97, 109
Laguépie 32
Laroque-de-Fa 41
Lastours 28, 118-119
Laurac 57
Lauragais 56-57
Lavaur 30-32, 56-57
Lavelanet 69, 75
Le Mas-d'Azil 70-71
Le Tuc d'Audoubert 70-71
Les Cassés 30-31, 57
Lézignan 9
Limousis Caves 117
Limoux 18, 106-107
Lombers 21, 26, 49
Lombrives Cave 73
Lordat 72-73
Lourdes 35-36

M

Magrin 57
Mas-Cabardès 20, 65
Mas-Saintes-Puelles 16, 57
Mazères 67
Miglos 72-73
Minerve 12, 122-123
Miramont Castle 92
Mirepoix 41, 64-65
Moissac 32
Montady Lake 125
Montaillou 67, 72-73, 95
Montauban 30, 32, 36, 41
Montégut 32
Montferrand 30
Montgaillard 36, 69
Montgey 57
Montolieu 41, 112
Montpellier 24-25
Montréal 26, 41, 63, 95
Montségur 42, 74-77
Muret 26, 33, 55, 67, 69, 127

N-P

Narbonne 126-127
Niaux Cave 70-71
Notre-Dame de Centeilles 121
Notre-Dame de Laval 85
Padern 92
Pamiers 26-27, 32, 67
Penne 41
Peyrepertuse 86-89
Pieusse 39, 103, 107
Port-la-Nouvelle 127
Portiragnes 9
Pouzols-Minervois 121

Preixan 26
Prouille 23, 63
Puilaurens 44, 82-83
Puivert 78-79
Puycelci 30
Puylaurens 26, 30, 32, 40, 57, 69

Q-R

Quercorb Museum 79
Quéribus 90-93
Rabastens 30, 32
Razès 104-105
Rennes-le-Château 104-105
Rennes-les-Bains 105
Rieux-Minervois 109, 121
Rocamadour 30-31
Roquefixade 68-69

S

Sabarthès 72-73
St-Antonin 30, 32
St-Bertrand-de-Comminges 33
St-Félix-Lauragais 20-21, 57
St-Ferréol 59
Saint Georges' Gorges 81
St-Germain-de-Cesseras 120-121
St-Gilles 15-16, 23-25, 29, 41, 54
St-Girons 71
St-Hilaire 108-109
St-Jean-de-Verges 40, 69
St-Lizier 36, 69
St-Paul-Cap-de-Joux 57
St-Marcel 32
St-Martin-des-Puits 96-97
St-Martin-Lys 81
St-Papoul 60-61
St-Paul-de-Fenouillet 85
St-Polycarpe 106-107
Saissac 116-117
Sallèles-d'Aude 127
Sarlat 21
Saverdun 33
Sérignan 125
Sigean 127
Servian 23

T

Tarascon-sur-Ariège 70-71, 73
Tautavel 84-85
Termes 100-101
Terminet Gorges 101
Tonneins 25
Toulouse 17, 18, 35-37, 52-55

U-V

Ussat 123
Usson 16, 76, 80-81
Valcabrère 33
Vals 66-67
Verfeil 21, 23, 95
Villelongue 116-117
Villeneuve-les-Corbières 9
Villerouge-Termenès 98-99